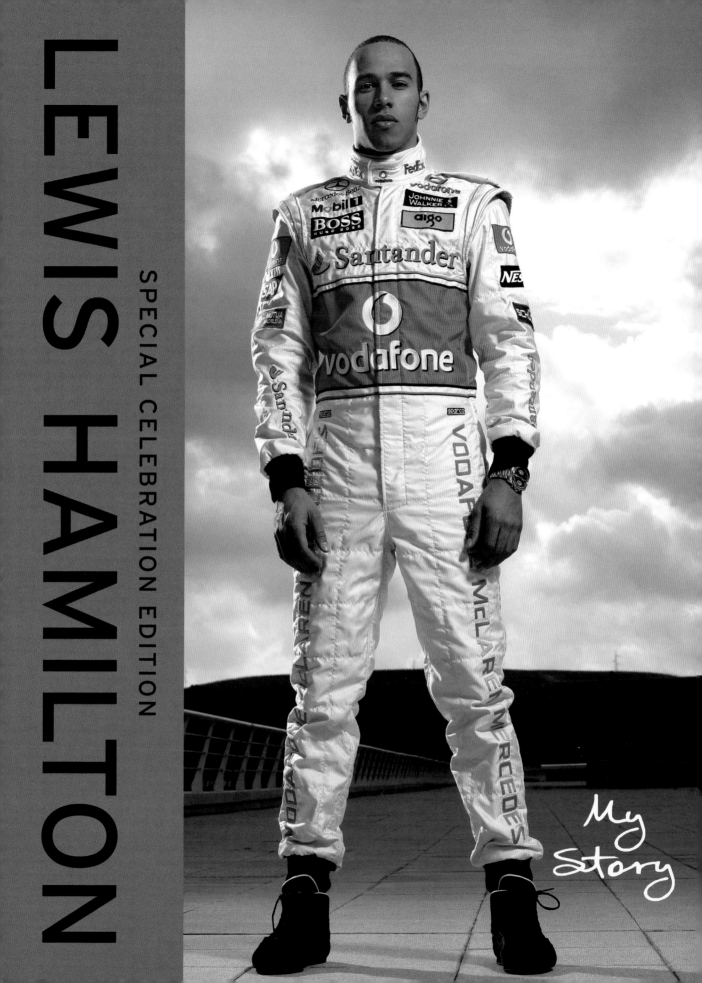

LEWIS HAMILTON

SPECIAL CELEBRATION EDITION

My Story

CONTENTS

WINNING   11

RESOLVE   27

INSPIRATIONS   35

CONFIDENCE   53

STARTING OUT   65

CLIMBING   79

DREAMS   93

RUNNING   103

Acknowledgements   218

Being world champion is an amazing feeling. It's the culmination of years of hard work and challenges, and my family and McLaren have been with me every step of the way.

Here is my story brought bang up to date.

WINNING

IT WAS PANDEMONIUM, BRAZILIAN-STYLE. I had just got out of the car and I was world champion. Everyone was going crazy. It was raining and I was looking all around. I still had my helmet on and I could not see my dad anywhere. There were people surrounding me, cameras in my face, someone pulling on my race suit and everybody shouting and jostling. I was still fighting to come to terms with it all.

I stepped from the car and ran towards some of my team and gave them a hug. Then I saw my brother and I gave him a big hug too. Somebody passed me a flag, the Union Jack, and I looked down to find the corners so I could hold it behind me. For what seemed like ages I still couldn't find my dad and was wondering where he was. Later I found out he was right at the front calling out to me but I couldn't see or hear him for all the excitement.

I started running down the pit lane to get back to the garage because I thought that might be where he was. There was a voice behind me but because of my helmet I could not hear properly. The voice kept calling and eventually I looked round. It was dad running alongside me. 'Lewis, any chance of a hug?' he shouted. Suddenly all the tension of the year slipped from my shoulders and I wrapped my arms around him. We'd done it, finally. We were world champions. What a moment that was!

It was crazy. Totally crazy. My mind was overflowing with emotions: elation, relief, tension, pure happiness. People keep asking me what winning a world championship actually feels like. It's this rollercoaster ride of emotions riding into one another. And above all there's an intense joy that just lifts your body and soul – and it doesn't go away.

The next morning, I woke up in my hotel room and it took another second to hit me. And then I just lay back and smiled and thought, 'Man, I did it. I'm a Formula One world champion!' I tell you, nothing in the world is better than that feeling ...

The joy of Brazil was a long way from the start of my season, which began back in January at the launch of our new car on a freezing winter's day in Stuttgart. It was only my second season in Formula One but I knew it was going to be an important year. I had a new team-mate, Heikki Kovalainen, there were new rules – electronic traction control had been banned at the end of the previous year – and I was now the most experienced racing driver in the team and would be expected to perform. There could be no excuses this time.

I knew what I was capable of achieving. Even without driver aids, our new car was a big step forward from the 2007 chassis and we spent those cold winter months really bonding as a team as we developed our package ahead of the first race of the season.

'It was only my second season in Formula One but I knew it was going to be an important year.'

Travelling to Australia we knew that Ferrari were probably our most serious rivals. We didn't count any of the other teams out of the running but we were pretty confident that we would be seriously competitive too. The first race of the year is always exciting because it answers so many of the questions you'd been asking yourself during the whole winter. Despite all the testing we do in January and February, you never quite know how competitive you're going to be because all your rivals are disguising their true pace.

I went on to win the Australian Grand Prix, the first race of the season. How crazy was that! It is an emotional race to win because it puts to bed a lot of the doubts that you'd had about your competitiveness. It's also good for everybody's morale – it pumps you up for the rest of the season. It's always been one of my targets to win the first race of the year and, even though Ferrari had run into difficulties, we felt comfortable that we were now going to be strong enough to fight for the title.

But things didn't get any easier in the next four races. Ferrari won them all and I made mistakes in Malaysia and also in Bahrain, where I crashed into the back of my old team-mate Fernando Alonso. I was happy to score some decent points in Spain and Turkey but I knew I needed another strong result to stay in the hunt for the world championship.

Going back to Monaco after coming so close last year put me in a very positive frame of mind for the whole weekend. I love Monaco – it's the greatest circuit in the world and the first track I began to recognise when I was a boy growing up and watching Formula One. Back then, I always used to associate it with Ayrton Senna, because he won there so many times, but it just looked like such a spectacular place on the television – with the casino, the tunnel and the swimming pool – that it quickly became my favourite race.

Race day was damp and rainy, and everybody was pretty cautious during the opening laps because it was very easy to make a mistake. I wasn't particularly pushing when I was sat behind Felipe, but on one lap I brushed my rear wheel against the barrier at the exit of a corner.

It was only a tiny mistake – I was just correcting a snap of oversteer – but the tyre punctured pretty quickly. That's Monaco for you, it punishes even the smallest of errors. And before I'd even got back to the pits the back-end of my car was fish-tailing about quite badly.

The pit crew filled my car up, changed my tyres and I rejoined the race without losing too much time. I couldn't believe I was able to get back in the race so quickly but I stayed focused, started pulling out some good laps and was able to establish a cushion at the front of the field.

Driving around Monaco is pretty special – it's so tight and so tough. When you first drive out of the pits on the Thursday morning you can't believe there's room in those streets for a Formula One car, but you quickly fall into a groove. Very quickly, it just feels easy. And Monaco is all about finding your rhythm; not pushing too hard too soon. I love it because there's no other circuit on earth where a Formula One car feels such a part of you; it's like the car and driver are almost joined together. And when you lock into the groove it just feels amazing.

Into the closing laps, I was still ahead. But I always tell myself that you can never think about winning until you've actually crossed the finish line. So I just kept my head, reeled off the laps and took the chequered flag. That's when it sunk in that I had just won the Monaco Grand Prix. I remember parking up on the start line and hugging my dad and my brother with tears in my eyes. I'd dreamt of winning this race since I was a small boy – and to achieve it driving for the same team as Ayrton Senna was hugely emotional for me. This victory was something pretty special to me.

I was still riding on the crest of a wave when I arrived in Montreal for the Canadian Grand Prix a fortnight later. I like the Circuit Gilles Villeneuve – it's where I won my first Formula One race in 2007 and it's a tricky place that usually throws up some unusual results. You've got to drive very carefully to win in Canada.

'I was still riding on the crest of a wave when I arrived in Montreal for the Canadian Grand Prix a fortnight later.'

I was on course to do just that until my accident in the pit lane. I'd just stopped for new tyres and was totally focused on getting back out in the lead. It all happened so quickly: I saw Robert and Kimi ahead of me, but somehow I thought they were fighting each other in the pit lane. I glanced up and saw the red light but by the time I looked down again, I just knew I wasn't going to be able to stop in time. I hit the brakes as hard as I could but still ran into the back of Kimi, putting us both out of the race.

I was gutted – not just for myself, but for the team – and for Kimi too. I said sorry to him at the time and I also contacted him after the race and apologized again. Kimi was very gracious. The incident in Canada earned me a ten-place grid penalty for the French Grand Prix in Magny-Cours. That race was another disaster as I finished out of the points.

Those two disappointing results meant that the buzz of winning Monaco all seemed a very long time in the past. The days after France, when I hadn't scored in the last two races, were probably the most difficult of my season. It was a low time. And the next race was the British Grand Prix so I knew I'd have to deliver the goods or else there would be some difficult explaining to do.

But instead of life getting harder, the weeks building up to my home race at Silverstone were some of the most positive of my life: I got to meet Nelson Mandela in London, which was something I'll never forget; I launched my Reebok ambassador campaign in Amsterdam; and I even spent an awesome day onboard the Hugo Boss boat as it raced around the Isle of Wight.

'In those slippery conditions, your concentration in the cockpit is so intense.'

All of a sudden, Silverstone seemed a lot easier to deal with. We'd tried out some new parts during the test the week before and the car suddenly felt amazing again. We were quick all weekend and right back in the hunt. So when it started to pour with rain on the Sunday morning, I knew we were in excellent shape for the race.

In those slippery conditions, your concentration in the cockpit is so intense: you feel every tiny snap through the steering wheel and you're poised to make a dozen split-second corrections. It's an insane way to drive, but the buzz is so awesome that it actually becomes quite relaxing.

And that's what happened at Silverstone; I just found a pace and rhythm where I was comfortable leading the race, and I stuck with it. Soon, the team came on the radio and told me to slow down, which was a bit weird because I definitely wasn't pushing. They told me the gap back to second place was growing. I remember it being 40 seconds, then 48 seconds – and it kept getting bigger. I couldn't understand it. 'Guys, if I go any slower I'll be going backwards!' I told them over the radio.

As I crossed the line, I felt this huge pressure lift off my shoulders. Ron came on the radio: 'That was a well-disciplined drive, Lewis – tremendous work.' Ron sounded calm, but I was almost screaming in the cockpit: 'Fantastic job, guys. Thank you so much for giving me your support – it's been a tough weekend but we've done it; we've bloody done it!'

It was one of the best races I've ever driven. In fact it was a pivotal race for me and the team and it resurrected our championship hopes. But the impact of that drive only really sank in at the end of the day when I walked on stage at Silverstone's Sunday evening concert in the centre of the circuit. I'll never forget the sound of the crowd roaring their support. I love the fans at Silverstone – they're the most passionate and knowledgeable in the world, and seeing all the flags waving and realizing that I'd helped make all those people happy was a crazy moment for me. Even better, I got to share the moment with Nic who came on stage with me and got a special cheer from the crowd. What a perfect way to end a fantastic day.

The season rolled on. I took another win in front of 100,000 cheering Mercedes-Benz supporters at Hockenheim, and two more podiums in Hungary and Valencia. I still held a six-point lead in the title fight but by September the championship was really starting to get close.

Sharing a joke
with my hero.

There were still four drivers in the hunt – myself, Felipe, Kimi and Robert – but it was clear to me that Felipe was emerging as my main challenger for the world title. He'd been dominant in Hungary and Valencia and was starting to build up some good momentum at Ferrari. But the next race was at Spa Francorchamps, one of my favourite tracks, and I felt pretty confident that our package would be very strong.

As it turned out, Kimi was the quickest Ferrari driver that weekend. I followed him for lap after lap during the race and simply had no answer to his speed. Into the last few laps, I came on the radio and told the team he was just too fast, that I couldn't catch him. They came back on the radio and said, 'Keep pushing Lewis – don't give up, there's rain on the radar and it's predicted to fall in the last three laps. Come on, you can do this!'

Our car is fantastic when the conditions are cold and damp and I knew this was my chance. Following Kimi, I could see he was starting to struggle for grip and I quickly pulled right onto his tail. Into the final chicane with only a couple of laps to go, he braked early on the inside line and I drew up alongside him into the braking zone.

We drove round that first right-hander together and he came into view, and I saw him creep alongside me before moving over as far as he could on the exit. I had nowhere to go and had to weigh up my options quickly. I knew if I turned right I was going to crash and take both of us out of the race. If I just slammed my brakes on, our wheels would have touched. I couldn't go over the kerb or the Astroturf, as they were wet and would have resulted in my losing control and crashing into Kimi. So I figured it was safer to steer left and miss the apex through the run-off on the chicane that was there for safety reasons. I let Kimi back past, before getting back to full throttle and passing him into La Source. He passed me again but then crashed out of the race and I was back in the lead. It was a fantastic victory – for the time being.

It was only after the podium ceremony that I was told the earlier manoeuvre was being investigated by the stewards of the meeting. I went to the stewards' office to explain what had happened but I just couldn't believe it when the team told me I'd lost my victory and been demoted to third. My team appealed against the stewards' decision and the whole thing ended up in the FIA court of appeal, but they didn't give their view on the decision or punishment because they said that type of penalty could not be appealed. Whatever the outcome, it was a fantastic race for me.

There had been a lot of talk among the drivers about racing under flood-lights around the streets of Singapore. As it turned out, the race and the circuit were both exceptional – the track was incredibly bumpy but very hot and demanding – and there were no real problems with the lights.

A Safety Car period probably cost me the chance of victory, but I wasn't too concerned because my main rivals failed to score and I was able to get some decent points for third place behind Fernando and Nico Rosberg – neither of whom were fighting me for the title.

'There had been a lot of talk among the drivers about racing under floodlights around the streets of Singapore.'

Still, we'd reached that point of the season where you really start to focus on the world championship. It's weird; although every race counts equally towards your final points' total, you definitely find yourself treating the races towards the end of the season far more importantly than the ones at the beginning. The tension definitely starts to rise and your ability to deal with that pressure becomes almost as important as what you're doing out on the track.

I felt pretty happy with my result in Singapore, but with three flyaway races at the end of the year to decide the title, I knew it would be important to be well prepared for the last stage of the championship. They would require long periods away from home and far from everything you feel familiar with. It's a big step to be away for so long, and, in times like these, I knew that I needed my family around me.

Our first stop was Japan. I won at the Fuji International Speedway in 2007 and I love the circuit, the food, the culture and the amazing people. After practice and qualifying I felt pretty confident that we'd be able to score another good result. Once again, however, things didn't go our way and my race was pretty much over after the first two laps.

I was on pole but I made a poor start as my clutch slipped – probably my worst start of the year – and I dropped behind Kimi on the run down to the first corner. I knew I'd have a chance to jump back ahead underbraking, but the cool temperatures and my cold brakes and tyres meant I was just a bit too optimistic. Half the field seemed to lock up or go wide underbraking for the first turn, but I made a mess of Turn One and Turn Three and was pushed down the pack, fighting with Felipe – who turned into me a lap later and nudged me into a spin. From then on, it was basically all over.

After the race I just wanted to crawl into a hole and disappear; I was so angry with myself. I got out of the car and marched straight back to the garage, got changed and started to walk out of the circuit. I just wanted to get as far away from the place as quickly as possible. Dad came and found me sitting in the car. We talked. He made a lot of sense – telling me to bottle my anger and go back and talk to the journalists who needed to know what had happened. I did it, and I'm glad I did – it taught me a few valuable lessons about dealing with disappointment and containing my feelings.

A few hours later we left for Tokyo. As soon as I got to the hotel, I went straight to my room and told everyone to leave me alone. It was not the first time in my career that I had felt I was at crisis point. But I believed, as I always have, that I had the strength to come back stronger. It was then that I decided to invite my two mums and my brother Nic to China. My family are vital in giving me the energy and belief when I need it.

I flew to Shanghai a few days later. I didn't spend too much time thinking about my race in Fuji – I just wanted to look forward and take any of that negative energy and turn it into a positive. The team were brilliant too. When I turned up at the circuit on Thursday, everybody was just filled with positivity and determination to strike back. That gave me a lot of energy too, and I just had this feeling it was going to be another good weekend.

The Chinese Grand Prix was an absolute dream for me: pole position, fastest lap and victory in the race. At such a critical point in the season, the win couldn't have come at a better time. And I worked incredibly hard to make sure I performed faultlessly – it's the only thing you can do when there is a lot of pressure around you.

I was really relaxed in Shanghai because my family came to watch the race. I hung out with Nic whenever I wasn't in the car – we'd play computer games or watch comedy DVDs in my room together. In my job, people don't get to see me laughing very much, but Nic is the one guy who always puts a smile on my face.

'The Chinese Grand Prix was an absolute dream for me: pole position, fastest lap and victory in the race.'

Linda and my mum Carmen made the trip out to China too. It was Mum's first race since Canada and I was really pleased that I didn't disappoint her this time. Afterwards I just remember squeezing both of them so tightly as we celebrated together – that weekend was definitely a special feeling for all of us.

I should also dedicate that race to my engineers and mechanics: in China we showed just how much you could achieve with a well-sorted car. They are a fantastic team and work so hard together and this was probably our strongest performance of the whole year. To be honest, the car never felt better than it did at Shanghai and I now felt really confident about the championship-decider in Brazil.

This time I was seven points ahead but I felt in a much better place than I did a year ago. Yes, I had more experience – and I had the luxury of having already been in a title-decider, something new to Felipe – but I think I knew in my head how I would deal with everything this time around.

Still, the atmosphere was quite weird in the team. We knew that even if Felipe won the race, we only had to finish fifth to clinch the world championship. We'd factored that into all our calculations, but it still felt strange going into a race aiming for fifth rather than a win. That sort of thing just wasn't in our vocabulary and meant we would be working to a strange rhythm throughout the weekend.

The team were desperate to take things steadily. We all knew we had come so close the previous year and there was no way we wanted to let the title slip through our fingers again. The engineers and mechanics had done all they could to make sure the car was reliable – a constant worry when you knew that Felipe was most likely going to win the race – and it was really drummed into me that I had to drive calmly, stay out of trouble and, above all, just keep the car on the track.

As I sat on the grid in Brazil, I felt strangely calm. I could hear the crowds in the grandstands chanting for Felipe but I knew I had plenty of opportunities to grab a good result. Then it started raining. Hard. The pit crews scattered, grabbing wet-weather tyres just minutes before the start. I didn't think you could make Sao Paulo any crazier, but that rainstorm had almost guaranteed the most important race of my life was going to be a lottery – and there was absolutely nothing I could do about it.

I didn't get a brilliant getaway on the wet track but, more importantly, it was a clean start and I kept out of trouble. We shadowed the leaders for most of the race and while I didn't attempt to trouble the guys ahead, I felt comfortable running in fourth or fifth because that was all I needed to do to claim the title. Besides, I was having trouble with my rear tyres and it would have been crazy to push harder and risk flat-spotting or puncturing them. I knew I just had to sit behind the leaders and stay calm.

Then it started to rain again. I couldn't believe it. The track got damp and slippery pretty quickly – in those moments you're desperate not to fall off, and you know that even the tiniest mistake can send you spinning off into the gravel.

I pitted for another set of wet-weather tyres and came out of the pits in fifth – just ahead of Sebastian Vettel in the Toro Rosso. Sebastian had already won in the rain at Monza so I knew that he had a good car in the wet, but I still felt comfortable keeping him behind. But my new tyres weren't working and I was struggling for traction. It soon got difficult just to keep Sebastian behind me. Out of the last corner on lap 68 I ran wide in the traffic and he shot up the inside and got past.

It felt like a flame had been snuffed out inside me. I just stared at the back of this Toro Rosso as it began racing up the hill. I was yelling, 'No, no, no!' to myself and knew I was back in sixth position and it wouldn't be enough to win the title. I desperately tried to get the power down and close back up to him, but the car was just getting more and more difficult to drive. The back-end kept snapping away and I just couldn't get any traction. Despite all my efforts, Sebastian was pulling away.

The team was on the radio again: 'Lewis, you are sixth. You must pass Vettel. You *must* pass Vettel.' They didn't need to tell me, I knew it. But it was impossible. The title was slipping away. Again! This couldn't be happening to me.

Into the last lap my heart was beating like crazy. I didn't even need to ask if Felipe was leading; the team hadn't told me but I knew he was going to win the race. Onto the back straight, I left my braking as late as possible but got another big slide at the exit. Sebastian grew smaller and smaller in front of me as he got further away.

I didn't have any grip.

I didn't have any time.

I didn't have any answers.

I kept pushing, even though I knew it was probably all over.

Then the team came on the radio again. 'Lewis, Glock is on dry tyres. He is struggling. If you can pass him you will be fifth. Don't focus on Vettel – just get past Glock.' I couldn't even see Timo so I didn't know what was happening. Then as we drove into Turn 10, just two corners from the finish, I could see this white Toyota at the exit of the corner – and it was struggling.

'Into the last lap my heart was beating like crazy. I didn't even need to ask if Felipe was leading.'

We raced out of Turn 11 and Sebastian just flew past Timo, who was now tiptoeing along. I saw my chance: the Toyota was about to turn into the final corner and I knew I had to get past right away or it would all be over.

My heart was exploding. I could hardly drive the car, the grip was nowhere and I was just desperate. I don't know how I kept my cool but I held my breath, lunged up the inside and pulled ahead of him. I was through!

By now my head was just numb and all I could do was make sure my exit was as neat as possible so I could out-accelerate Timo up the hill. Then the thoughts started rushing into my head. Had I done enough? I wasn't completely sure because wet races can be so chaotic. My head was hurting, my brain was pounding and my heart was going crazy. I was sure the team was going to come on the radio at any second and explode with joy that I'd got fifth, but there was nothing. Absolutely nothing. I didn't know what was happening. I flicked on the radio and kept shouting over and over again: 'Do I have it? Do I have it?'

'The 2008 season has been one of the most intense and exciting years of my life.'

I took the flag and started to slow down. What was happening? What on earth was happening? My heart could barely take the strain. Suddenly the radio crackled on – and it seemed to take about a million years for a voice to start speaking. One of my engineers said: 'You're P5, you've done it!' I don't think it really sank in until immediately afterwards. Phil Prew, my race engineer, followed up with: 'Congratulations Lewis, you are the 2008 Formula One World Champion!'

Words cannot describe how I felt then. I was just choked by it all. I started yelling and screaming in the car. I wanted to cry. I wanted to jump out of the cockpit. I could hardly breathe – it felt like I had been holding my breath for the last four laps with my heart in my mouth. Even when I got the car back

We did it! I was the world champion: the Formula One World Champion!

to the pit lane and climbed out, I could still hardly move. I was trembling and fumbling. I was numb – I had a million emotions flowing through me all at once. I'd never felt anything like it in my life before.

Faces flashed before me: my dad, Linda, my brother, Nicole – she was crying and laughing at the same time. Everybody was looking to me. Nobody could stop smiling. It was simply overwhelming – we'd come so far and won it in the last few seconds. I was the world champion – the Formula One World Champion!

One of the best ways of keeping my feet on the ground was to immediately head back to Woking, to the McLaren Technology Centre, to meet everyone who had worked so hard to help win this championship. When I arrived, I just thought it was going to be a regular visit, but the team suddenly threw a pair of overalls at me and strapped me into my Formula One car in the staff car park.

I blasted around the lake at the front of the building in my racecar and was greeted by the sight of 1,000 people cheering me home all dressed in the red victory T-shirts we wear after winning a grand prix.

I parked up at the main entrance and jumped out of the car and started waving to everyone. I was finally in front of all the people who had worked their butts off for me and the race team, and this was a small chance for me to say thank you to all of them. During the rest of the week, I also made sure I went to Mercedes-Benz in Brixworth and Stuttgart and to the Vodafone HQ to do the same thing.

That is why I feel so much pride at winning this championship – not for myself, but for my dad, my family, everyone in my team and for my country. I love the feeling of putting a smile on everybody's face.

The 2008 season has been one of the most intense and exciting years of my life. Winning the world championship has opened up a whole new world to me. And while I will keep my feet on the ground, I can't help feeling that the words 'Lewis Hamilton, Formula One World Champion' just sound so cool. Better than I could ever have imagined ...

RESOLVE

MY STORY IS NOT ABOUT LUCK OR A FAIRY TALE. It is about hard work, about my family's sacrifices and determination, my dad's huge support for me and many other people's belief and kindness. I found I had a talent and I have worked as hard as possible to develop it so that I can be successful and in the process inspire others, if I can, to achieve a dream.

My first year in Formula One, 2007, was the most exciting and challenging of my life. From the start in Melbourne, which seems so long ago now, to the finish in São Paulo, I had a phenomenal year, winning four races, finishing as runner-up in five, and battling for podium finishes in a few others, in my rookie season with the Vodafone McLaren Mercedes team.

That I led the championship from the third race of the season all the way to the last was an amazing feat in itself, even if it meant the final outcome was tinged with some disappointment. I soon got over that, though – thanks to my dad's endless positive energy and example, and the McLaren team's great spirit, not to mention a memorable team party organized by Vodafone on the Sunday night after that final race at Inter-lagos. It summed up our unity at the end of a very trying season and I admit I enjoyed the opportunity to let my hair down a bit with my friends and team-mates.

I ended the season with good vibes. I felt proud of the team for the way they had worked through to the end of a really difficult, troubled year. The São Paulo party was good for us all. Ron Dennis made a speech and said some really good things and we had a great evening. It just rounded off the whole year and, when I was mentioned a couple of times, it made me feel proud to be part of that team.

So much happened to me in such a short a space of time that, when the season ended, I felt like I needed to stop, look back and take stock of what had happened. But in Formula One there is no time for that. The search for progress is relentless, the appetite for success, improvement and frontier-breaking unquenchable. Stand still for a moment and your rivals will pass you. That is the competitive nature of the sport. It comes out in every aspect of all of the teams' activities. Nothing is left to chance, no stone left unturned, in pursuit of greater speed, efficiency and effectiveness in all areas of a racing team. And that restlessness reflects the way I have always felt about my life in racing. I always want to move on and on, to keep going forward to the next level and the next challenge. But I always want to succeed properly, fair and square, out on the track and not in any other way.

'Stand still for a moment and your rivals will pass you.'

I had arrived in São Paulo in October 2007 leading the championship by four points, but I left in second place, just a single point behind the new champion Kimi Räikkönen. I may have been hit by mechanical problems, but I was beaten fair and square on the Interlagos track by Kimi and his Ferrari. It was no time for recriminations or complaints. I do not believe in doing that; I do not blame my team when things happen. We all win and lose together. Kimi drove superbly and won six races in all, including three out of the final four Grands Prix. He deserved his success. That is why I was quick to congratulate him at the end of the race in the *parc fermé*. I felt sore for myself, but I felt happy for Kimi – he is a cool guy and he had been a great competitor all year.

I had just finished my rookie year at the age of 22. I knew I had a future in Formula One and, with reasonable luck, plenty more opportunities to win the World Championship. I had no doubt about that. It had been a fantastic season and instead of feeling down, or in any kind of pain, I felt we had a lot to celebrate and enjoy. I felt proud of the way the team had come through a sometimes stormy, controversial year and I felt proud, too, of my family and all my friends and supporters who had helped me to get where I was, so close to the title in my first season. It was a day to be happy. In the end, the year was not decided by that one race in Brazil, but a whole championship season.

If somebody had told me twelve months earlier that I would be fighting for the World Championship at the end of the 2007 season, I would have said they were dreaming. But that is what happened. In the end, I lost by just one point, but I proved I had the potential to be involved in more and more championship fights in the future. Nobody would have predicted that I would finish second in my first season, so there was no reason for anything but celebrations. I did my best, the team did their best and there was nothing any of us could do to change things. In all honesty, at the end, I just felt it had been a really intense, crazy year and, truly, I did not feel gutted by the outcome. I believed in the team and the car, and I was looking ahead with real optimism.

Who would have thought I would be leading the 2007 World Championship going into the last race? Who could have imagined the crowds we had at Silverstone for the British Grand Prix? Who would have dreamt that I would go to North America and win back-to-back Grands Prix in Canada and the United States? Or win four races and start from pole position six times in 17 races?

'If somebody had told me twelve months earlier that I would be fighting for the World Championship at the end of the 2007 season, I would have said they were dreaming.'

I know it was all against me in the end, and that the final two races were bad results for me, but I planned to learn from that and tried to improve all round. I was determined to come back fitter, more relaxed and more experienced – and I knew I would have a better car and would push harder for the championship. To think I came straight from GP2 to be ranked number two in the world is a positive thing and I knew we would only get stronger. We would do a better job, for sure, that the team would keep pushing and that I had got the experience now and I would bank that. I couldn't wait for the next race! Of course, I felt emotional afterwards in Brazil, at least a little bit. I try not to show emotions, but I cannot deny that I felt it a little when the season ended.

When I think back, there are so many great memories: my GP2 Championship, then the opportunity to test for the Vodafone McLaren Mercedes team and those early tests at Silverstone and at Jerez in September and October 2006. They were just a year before the title-decider in Brazil. I remember that first week of testing at Silverstone when I wore some other dude's race suit to start with, and it smelt. When I got my own, I thought it was so cool, I wanted to sleep in it! The whole journey for me, from my earliest days as part of the McLaren and Mercedes-Benz family to Formula One, has been quite emotional.

The test at Silverstone – only a year before I flew to Japan and China for the two Grands Prix that lifted me within reach of my first title and then dashed my hopes – was the best week of my life at the time. I enjoyed it so much. I felt the pressure because it was my first test and I wanted it to be right. The thing that really struck me, after GP2, was the downforce in the high-speed corners. I was like, 'Wow, this is Formula One! I want this!' And then I went to Jerez to test again, and gradually, after not such a fast start, I was into my stride and doing the laps. I just loved that testing and it went well and, looking back now, I have only good memories.

It seems so long ago. So, too, does the day I was confirmed as Fernando Alonso's team-mate, as a race driver in the team, and all the other testing. And the launch in Valencia on 15 January in my debut season, when we did all the razzmatazz and had those huge crowds and did the 'doughnuts' in the streets . . . So much has happened since – and luckily for me, nearly all of it has been good. One of the few bad days came when I had a big accident testing the new MP4-22 at Valencia before the season. Fortunately for me I was unhurt, but the car was quite badly damaged and it set us back in our test programme. That accident was a shaker for me, a reminder of what these cars can do, and it was a big part of my early learning experience with the team.

In fact I have learned something every day since. I am so competitive that I always want to achieve more and more. It is a positive force for me. I want to win. I have to always be realistic and remember that it was my first season and it was something special for me. I was bound to make some mistakes. I started out just hoping to learn a lot, to challenge Fernando and to prove I was worthy of my seat in the team. The level of expectation was a measure of how far I had gone in that space of time.

'It is not so much about doing things differently but doing them better. Learning from other people's mistakes as well as my own.'

After Brazil 2007, I was asked if there was anything different I would do for the following season given my experiences in my first year. A lot of things, really. I had the experience to know how to plan my year differently so I could be more structured and have more time for myself and for my family. I had experience of the circuits. It is not so much about doing things differently but doing them better. I wanted to be fitter, work harder and be a better driver all round. I knew all of this was not something that could be achieved overnight, as it takes time to evolve – especially if you are striving to become the best in the world. My dream was still there. So in one way, maybe it was a good thing that I wasn't crowned number one in 2007. It may have been too much too soon, but in any case I moved on and prepared for 2008.

I find it easy to overcome negativity, but disappointment can occasionally take a little longer. Life goes on and every new day is a new positive. Sometimes, you just have to say to yourself, 'Get on with it.' I am my own biggest critic and often want to say, 'Lewis, kick it!' I push myself. It is the same for us all in the team and we work for each other, helping one another as much as we can. A racing team is not just about the person who is driving the car. It is much, much bigger than that. I have been very lucky to have learned a lot from the Vodafone McLaren Mercedes team. I have gained so much from driving and handling the car, set-up, tyre selection, strategy and the whole range of factors that can make a driver successful.

I have also learned a lot about the politics of Formula One . . .

INSPIRATIONS

TO BE A FORMULA ONE RACING DRIVER you need to be extremely fit and prepared – both physically and mentally – for the whole challenge. It is far more exhausting than you can ever imagine if you have never raced in a car. And it is not easy. Sometimes, if you are not feeling right, if you do not have the right energy levels, it can be impossible. It is important to find your own way, then keep your mind clear and maintain the right level of motivation.

Just the ordinary things – like travelling all the time; packing bags, grabbing them and taking them with you; going to functions, meeting people; the crowds, the heavy schedule – all take their toll on your energy and strength after a while. So it is important to stay calm when you can and not to waste energy.

I have a special source of extra motivation. For me, even when I am feeling pretty stretched, rushing around in the middle of a Formula One weekend and surrounded by people who want a bit of my time – and with what feels like a thousand things to do – I only have to think of one person to keep me feeling motivated and to put a smile on my face: my brother Nicolas. I remember Linda, my step-mum, being pregnant with Nic. I remember him being born and that I would just go and sit next to him and watch him. I had prayed to have a brother and was so happy when he came into the world. It really meant a lot to me, in my childhood, to have a brother. And it still does.

Nic was born two months early and it was a long time after his birth – I think nearly eighteen months – before he was diagnosed with cerebral palsy. He was still the same Nic to us and we loved him whatever. Nic has trouble walking, and this affects his whole body to a point, but he never complains. He always has a smile on his face whatever the situation.

I remember when Nic was four he had to have an operation on his legs to extend the tendons so as to increase his mobility. The operation was a major one and very distressing. Nic had to have cuts in his groin, behind his knees, and in his ankles. He was in plaster for about eight weeks. I was only eleven and heavily into my karting by then, going to race tracks at weekends and having a great time. We always went to every race as a family – Linda, Nic, my dad and me. Nic was let out of hospital after about a week and they gave him this little wheelchair. As soon as he was released, Nic was back on the racing circuit with us, his legs stretched out straight in front of him and plastered up to the groin. The whole operation period was a very traumatic time for us all, in particular Nic, who, when the time came to take off his plaster casts, thought the doctors were going to cut his legs off! I remember he cried his eyes out but it wasn't long before that smile came back to his face. That smile – it is infectious and inspirational. It taught me a lot about life. Nic has always been my number one fan and I am his.

I just hope that by writing about him, he doesn't get too big-headed because, if he does, I will have to make sure I bring him back down to earth by beating him on the computer games! He is such a character, so grounded too, and he is always cheerful and happy. He has big respect from me and all who know him. Nic is seven years younger than me and because of that, I sometimes feel like I have to set an example for him to follow, like my dad did for me. But most of the time, I am learning stuff from him.

Nic is now seventeen and, if anything, we are even closer. I love spending time with him. We enjoy the same sort of things, the same sort of music. As he gets older, it's good to be able to talk about girls with him! It won't be long before we can go partying together – and I am dying for the time when he is old enough so we can go out to a club or just do our own thing. That is going to be so cool.

It is rare for me during the season to get a decent period of time at my parents' home to spend with Nic but we did have a few in 2007. After the Turkish

Grand Prix, for example, and before I had to travel to Italy, I went home to my parents' house in Hertfordshire. The weather was great, Nic was there and we had fun doing all kinds of things together.

We played golf one day, for example. Nic finds it extremely difficult to stand still and balance in one place; add to that the fact that he is also left-handed, which does not help his swing. Even though he shouldn't be able to, Nic still attempts to play football, basketball, almost everything. He just never gives up and always puts 100 per cent effort into trying something even if he knows it's too much for him. Nic gets out of life what he puts into life and that must give him a huge amount of satisfaction. I know that he cannot do things as well as me but he has a real good go at it and makes me work even harder to make sure I beat him. 'Never let him have it easy,' is what my dad always said, just so that he would try harder. I am lucky in that I am good at most sports, but for Nic it must be really difficult. Either way, he always puts a smile on my face – although occasionally he can be quite argumentative. He reminds me of myself!

I often try to imagine myself in Nic's position. I do not think I would be anywhere near as strong as him. There's just so much to admire in him. So, whatever I am doing, I say to myself, 'If you think it's hard to do this, then think again.' I think about Nic's strength of character and that gives me added strength. So Nic is my inspiration – and that helps me a lot. But, in fact, my whole family are very close. We do everything we can together, and we always have done, but as I grow older and become more independent each year, I know that is probably going to change a bit – but not all that much. We have an intense bond and are a strong family. It helps us remain as normal as possible, to stay focused on the right things and not be distracted by all the stuff going on around us. We are a team, my family. We always have been. I like to think of my parents' home as my safe haven, the place where I can go to seek support, rest and reassurance in the good things in life.

Thanks to my family, I know it is important not to lose perspective – though at times in my career, that has not been easy. Formula One is such a demanding and fast-moving business that it is easy to lose your own sense of direction sometimes. It can be very, very tough so you have to

concentrate fully on the job in hand, prepare well and stay as level-headed and consistent as you can. If you stick to your beliefs and your true values in life, I believe things work out right in the end.

My mum Carmen and dad Anthony divorced when I was about two and I lived with my mum until I was ten. After that I moved to live with my dad and step-mum Linda. My mum is a huge and important part of my life and has always been there in the background wishing me success from afar. My step-mum Linda has been amazing and I think she is the best step-mum in the world. I was very emotionally attached to my dad, and it was difficult only seeing him at the weekends. They were the greatest weekends – I would not have missed them for anything – but I remember when I was ten that I liked living with my mum because she was the 'easier' parent.

You know with parents when you have the easy one and the demanding one? Well, she was the easier one. I've been extremely lucky: both my mum and Linda are incredibly considerate, very caring and generous, and fun-loving.

'He is my biggest supporter, and a fantastic father, without whom I may not have even discovered I had any talent for racing.'

A huge part of my personality – the emotional side, I would say – comes from both my mums. Even though my dad always told me, 'You have to be polite,' that was already in my nature. I would say my stronger, more competitive side comes from my dad. My selfishness, my focus, my determination, my ability to put things out of my mind, the way I say things and express myself, present myself well, and everything that gives people their perception of me – that all comes from, and has been driven by, my dad.

For example, my approach to things is: do not waver, never give up. My dad reminds me of that nearly every single day and I am always aware of how much work we have put in to get where we are today – and how much more work he expects me to do in the future! He is as relentless in his own way as I am in mine and I am sure that is a part of our characters that has contributed to our achievements. We are both hard workers and we believe in the same things – honesty, loyalty and trust – and we both have a never-say-die attitude. Anyone who knows him will tell you that. He is my biggest supporter, and a fantastic father, without whom I may not have even discovered I had any talent for racing! And he is a big reason – really the absolute reason – that I have been able to develop myself as a racing driver, and, probably more importantly, as a human being.

I am very close to my roots – to my father's family in Grenada, West Indies, where my real home is, and to the Grenadian people. My granddad lives in Grenada and drives a private minibus. His passengers are predominantly school children but my granddad will give just about anyone a lift. He is supposed to charge per ride but he just loves his job so much that sometimes he allows some passengers to ride for free. All the kids love him and out of respect they call him 'Uncle Dave', although his real name is Davidson. Nearly everyone in Grenada knows Uncle Dave. Wherever he goes people always acknowledge him and call out 'Uncle Dave!' He is everyone's uncle! My dad bought my granddad a new 18-seater minibus about a year ago because the old one was over twenty-five years old and my dad feared for the safety of my granddad and the passengers. I think my granddad's friends couldn't believe it. Some people didn't want to ride in Uncle Dave's old minibus because it was too slow but now everyone wants to ride in his new one.

'Every mistake and every good thing that has happened to me has counted.'

I feel close to all of that. I love Grenada; it is a beautiful country and a place where I have learned a lot. Living in multicultural Europe, it is easy to take things for granted, while in Grenada some people still live in buildings that resemble sheds. We visit Grenada every year, sometimes twice a year, and during our visits I get a real perspective on things, a better understanding of life altogether – and I realize how blessed I am. My family, my roots, and our values are primarily Grenadian, although we are British, having been born

in the UK. My granddad came to England in the 1950s and then returned to Grenada in the seventies following the death of my grandmother. My dad has always expressed a wish to return and I plan to do the same at some stage in my life but not now. To see the kids in Grenada with smiles on their faces – even if they've got very, very little in comparison with European kids – helps me to understand and manage my way in life. So my principles are always to listen to my dad, cherish my family, compete hard and never give up. Most of all, I try to keep a smile on my face.

Alongside the great experiences in my life I've also had some very bad, really challenging times – which you will read about later – but even those have made me stronger. And, with the help of my family, I've bounced back twice as strong as before. I think that is why I am probably such a strong character in racing. Every mistake and every good thing that has happened to me has counted. And there is not a day gone by that I wished I had done more of this or that. The way I see it, you have to rise above things and move on. You just cannot wait around. You have to do it yourself and just get on with it if you want things to happen.

'Alongside the great experiences in my life I've also had some very bad, really challenging times.'

That is why I feel like I have got such a responsibility to make people happy, make younger kids more determined or ambitious and to believe in hope and a dream. For me that is a pleasure: it is not just about the racing; it is all those other things that come into it that I really, really enjoy. I do occasionally pray – my granddad is very religious, he goes to church every day and he is always on my case, asking, 'Are you praying?' or telling me, 'Not to worry, Lewis, the Lord will provide, just ask for His help.' Every now and then I will say a prayer and show my appreciation. I try to make sure it is not only when I am in trouble and I need help; even when I have had a great day, I try to thank God for it.

That is why religion is not an issue for me – any more than race is an issue. I am Roman Catholic; I was baptized when I was two and for a lot of

Meeting David Coulthard at the McLaren Mercedes Young Driver Support Programme in 1998.

my life I always thought there was something there. Sometimes, if I was in trouble I would pray, but I was never hardcore into it – but then neither was the family, although we all believe. I have always felt very much that I have been gifted and very much blessed – I have a great family, a talent which many people don't either get to discover or experience, and I really do feel like there is a higher power and that He has given me something. Whether it is to send a message out, or to use, or just to have fun, I do not know. I think everyone has got talent and gifts, but not everyone discovers them, and people can occasionally be misled. I am fortunate that I have not been. I feel everyone is put here for a purpose and all the individuals that do discover things in their life are able to make a change and make a difference.

Some people think race, or skin colour, is an issue; some think religion is. Putting it simply, I do not like to see anyone treated badly. I do not like people who do not behave well, who are not polite or who do not show respect when they should. I guess it comes from my own younger days when I had to do things and I didn't find it easy. I had a bad time at school because there were some bullies around who were probably jealous of me going karting at weekends; either that or they just didn't like me. I tried to deal with that by defending myself, so I learned karate. That is my way of sorting out my problems. I try not to get entangled, I prefer to rise above them, but sometimes you need to be able to stand your ground, don't you? I believe in doing things right and doing them properly.

'I have huge respect for David [Coulthard]. He is a real gent and he taught me something good – that it costs nothing to say "Hello".'

I had a lot of other experiences when I was young, some good, some bad, but from each of them I learned something. In 1997, when I was thirteen, I went to my first Grand Prix at Spa-Francorchamps in Belgium. My dad and I were having a great day as guests of McLaren Mercedes. I remember walking around with my dad and we saw Eddie Irvine and decided to go and ask him for his autograph. I stood there in admiration of him, waiting for him to sign my book, but he looked at me and just walked on. It may well have been that Eddie was incredibly busy and did not have the time to be distracted or that he was just having a bad day. As a Formula One driver, with all the pressures on our time and our commitments, I now understand, but as a young kid I was kind of upset that he did not see me. I have never forgotten how that made me feel.

I met some of the other Formula One drivers that weekend. One of the nicest was David Coulthard. I was standing at the front of the McLaren garage when David came in and walked straight past me and my dad. I called out, 'Alright, David?' and he turned round and, two seconds later, he said, 'Alright, Lewis?' He knew me . . . what a feeling that was! I had met David previously when he came to a kart race meeting and he remembered me. I really appreciated it. So, always, I have huge respect for David, Eddie and all the other drivers. Each driver has different stresses and ways of dealing with the weekend. I want to make people happy, and so my policy is that it costs nothing to say 'Hello'.

I loved it at Silverstone, where I won the GP2 race in 2006.

I can say now that these two experiences certainly made me determined that if, or when, I reached the top and anyone ever asked me for an autograph, or a piece of my time, I will try to give them my time with good grace and respect. That is why I work hard to look after my many fans. I appreciate that's not always going to be easy or possible, but that's what I aim to achieve.

'It was not a good feeling ignoring the fans, doing the one thing I promised I would never do.'

Actually, it was not until Formula Three that I realized that I had fans, people that admired me for what I did. When they wanted to come over and talk to me, it was just a pleasure for me. All of them were polite to me, and I was no one as far as I was concerned, but they were always there supporting me. I was not used to that, but I learned from it. I have got some great fans all over the world, including those who come all the way from Japan, just for a weekend, to watch me race! I always try to make time for them because from past experiences I know how important it is to make time for others.

When I got to GP2, I noticed that my time was getting more precious – but I made sure I had enough of it to go around and say thank you to everyone. When I reached Formula One, it got more and more difficult, but I knew to expect this, so when I went to my first Grand Prix, in Australia, I said to myself that I must make time for the fans. I worked out that if I planned to get to the track at eight, and that I had a meeting starting at half past eight, then there was not enough time, in that half an hour, to start signing autographs. So I said to myself, 'I'll get there at 7.30 and use that extra time to sign auto- graphs.' What a great feeling it was to make others happy; that's a bit more energy in my energy bank. But I remember one day at Albert Park when I was just trying to juggle all the different events that were going on – I had a tyres briefing, an engineering meeting, and several other meetings and then I had to rush back to the hotel to do a HUGO BOSS and a Mercedes-Benz event, or something – and I was panicking. It all got to me. I didn't know how to judge it. I didn't have time to do autographs at the exit gate, where everyone was waiting outside the paddock, and I just walked on, and I kept walking. It was not a good feeling ignoring the fans, doing the one thing I promised I would never do. That was one of the single most distressing experiences I have ever had and it played on my mind all night.

'In my family we are all competitive and nobody likes to lose.'

So, next day, I made sure that I got a load of photos and posters and I signed about a hundred posters or more. I put 'Sorry' or 'Thank you' or something like that on them, and then the following day I went in early and signed a load of autographs as well and gave each person a poster. It felt good – I got all my energy back. A lot of fans who get the opportunity to come up close are sometimes physically shaking with nerves and I remember feeling it was incredible that I could make anyone feel that way. I'm only human. I'm not

Family video – Dad, Linda, Nic and me.

this big superstar that you see on TV. I am nothing special. I might be a Formula One racing driver, but that does not make me any different. As far as I am concerned we are all on the same level. I want to take time out of my schedule to sign an autograph if it is going to make someone's day. Making people happy is what makes me happy.

I do not believe in doing anything wrong to succeed. Never. In my family we are all competitive and nobody likes to lose. I would say my dad's the worst. He taught me how to win and lose but even he would admit that losing is not a nice experience to deal with – it does make your desire to succeed even stronger, though I can see how difficult he finds it some-times. It shows in his face, of course, even after a game of pool at home. And I can see it sometimes after races. We are alike, too, in that we stick to the same way of doing things. As I said earlier, we believe in the basics – honesty, loyalty and trust – and that is why we all found the politics in Formula One so hard to handle. As I said at the time, politics sucks.

'I love being at home with my family and the equilibrium that gives me.'

In my own way, the only thing to do was to rise above it all, concentrate on the racing, continue to do my best and, most important of all, keep a smile on my face which, with everything kicking off, had been difficult. All my lessons in life, my dad's and my family's advice and encouragement and examples of how to live and how to behave, have stood me in good stead. When you have been through some of the stuff I went through as a kid, living and growing up in a council house, which was great at the time, and when you have seen life through a really normal pair of eyes in Stevenage, in London, in Grenada and other places – all of that, on top of my early kart racing career, gave me the right kind of grounding to cope with it. So I just did my thing.

Being able to control yourself, redeem yourself, is important. When I play computer games with Nic I always try my best to beat him. I never let him win. I never let anyone win at anything, at home or anywhere, although sometimes, just sometimes, I do lose. I am always the same. I am just that competitive.

I have to win at everything, but I would never cheat. I just love knowing that I won fair and square or that I tried my best.

Mental strength is so important. On the surface, it may look like I am pretty calm most of the time, but underneath I am a very emotional person. That is why these things matter. I love being at home with my family and the equilibrium that gives me. We are all emotional people in my family – that is part of our nature – but in this business, in Formula One, you have to be a bit cold and a bit selfish. I suppose we are all a bit selfish in our own lives and that comes out sometimes in all of us. But I find I can balance it all if I am around my family.

Racing takes up most of my weekends, so any weekends I do have off are so important and valuable to me, and, going back to square one, returning to my own home and occasionally going to my parents' house, the safe haven – that is important, too. It is where I do all my mental preparation and feel good. My strength is in the family, wherever we all are, as long as we are together.

There are loads of places where you can get mental strength and energy, but again there are loads of places you can lose energy! Sometimes if I read negative press, it can consume loads of positive energy. So now I don't bother reading it. Neither does my dad, so he never passes negative energy on to me. My dad says it is part of his responsibility to protect me and absorb all the negative energy when it happens.

'For me, loyalty matters. In terms of friendship, it means being someone others can trust.'

This whole thing about changing negative energy into positive energy is not rocket science. It is just about trying to look on the positive side and turn anything negative into something positive. Occasionally, some things can become a huge distraction, but I have learnt to deal with this. A problem shared by talking to the people you love or care for is definitely the best way forward. That is where my family and friends come in.

I have been racing since I was eight years old and I have learned what works for me. I always try to remember to appreciate the opportunity I've been given and I always give 100 per cent. I always say, 'Keep your family and friends as close as possible.' These are the things I believe in and they have done me well.

In my career, it is the same. McLaren and Mercedes-Benz have been incredibly loyal to us and, hopefully, we will be loyal to them and I'll see out my career with them. For me, loyalty matters. In terms of friendship, it means being someone others can trust. And that works both ways.

I know I am a lucky person. I have a good life, I have been blessed with a talent and I have enjoyed myself very much, for most of the time, in my twenty-three years. It is never easy though. No way. Not for me, not for my dad and not for my family. We have had some extremely hard times and some extremely good times. But – and I think this is the most important thing – we have learned from them all and remained together and strong.

CONFIDENCE

MY START IN LIFE WAS PRETTY NORMAL. I was born at the Lister Hospital in Stevenage, Hertfordshire, on 7 January 1985. I was named Lewis Carl Davidson Hamilton. My dad's middle name is Carl and Nic also has Carl as a middle name. The name Lewis was just a name that my parents liked at the time. The name Davidson is taken from my granddad.

Stevenage was one of the 'new towns' built after the Second World War and is a typical commuter town with both local and international business facilities and good rail and road links to London, in the south, and to the north of England. Thousands of people travel from Stevenage to London and back every day on the train and my dad was one of them. He worked for British Rail while my mum worked in the local council offices. My mum and dad lived in a council house in Peartree Way, on the Shephall Estate, in Stevenage. My mum had two daughters – Samantha and Nicola – from a previous relationship before she met my dad. Sammy and Nicky were about two and three when my dad came into their lives. It was not a luxurious or a privileged neighbourhood, but it was also not as bad as some.

My first school was just down the end of our road, the Peartree Spring Nursery School. My second primary school, Peartree Infant and Junior School, was a five-minute walk around the corner. For my secondary school I chose the John Henry Newman School, a Roman Catholic secondary, before completing my education at the Cambridge Arts and Sciences College. I have to say it was not as straightforward as it sounds, and there were a few ups and downs along the way. My interest in karting and motor racing, which took me away a lot at weekends as I grew older, did not always fit in with the strict thinking of some people. At school, I used to keep my interest in racing to myself.

My racing career may not have started properly until I was eight, but it had in fact been part of my life much earlier. As a teenager, sadly my enthusiasm was not shared by all and my career nearly ended before it had started because of a case of mistaken identity by my secondary school.

To this day, I find it difficult to talk about this because it nearly destroyed my faith in the education system. But I think it's important to set the record straight on a few things in my life that have been reported inaccurately over the last couple of years or so.

It was 2001, I was sixteen and a few important months away from sitting my GCSEs at John Henry Newman School. In January of that year there was a serious incident at the school involving a pupil who was attacked in the school toilets by a gang of about six boys. I was accused of kicking the pupil. This was not true. I, like many others, had been hanging around waiting for the next lesson to start and had entered the toilets around the time that the attack was taking place. I was not involved in the attack but knew the boys involved.

My first run in a kiddie-kart during a family holiday in Ibiza in August 1988, aged three.

CONFIDENCE 57

The headteacher thought differently and wrote a letter to my parents advising them that I was excluded from school along with six other pupils and stating the reasons why. At the time I couldn't believe it. I was so upset. I didn't know how I was going to explain it to my parents. I walked around in a daze, not really knowing where I was going for a while, I even considered running away and then eventually I went home. When I gave the letter to my dad and step-mum Linda they were obviously extremely disappointed and really mad – not so much with me but with the headteacher – although I remember my dad said to me, 'Congratulations, you've done something that I never managed to do!' I knew that I had done nothing wrong so this made it all the worse.

'From the very beginning I told my dad that I was innocent and he did everything he could to prove this.'

We decided to go back to the school. I went with Linda and my mum to speak to the headteacher. When they arrived at the school, the headteacher did not appear sympathetic or very interested in anything they said to him and he maintained that I had kicked the pupil and that I was correctly excluded. I knew I was innocent and my parents knew that too. Subsequent letters to the local education authority, our local MP, the Education Secretary and even the Prime Minister were of no help. No one appeared to listen – no one either wanted to or had the time. We were on our own and I was out of school.

I found it very frustrating and upsetting, with everyone seemingly against me except my family, some true friends, and McLaren and Mercedes-Benz. I could not understand how I found myself in such an awful situation.

We launched an appeal to the Governors' Discipline Committee of the school, but the appeal failed. We then appealed to the Local Education Authority where the matter was considered by an independent Exclusion Appeal Panel.

From the very beginning I told my dad that I was innocent and he did everything he could to prove this. It was just typical of my dad: when something is wrong he will go to the ends of the earth to find out the truth.

Anyway, it took weeks to resolve (although it seemed so much longer at the time) with documents going backwards and forwards between the parties. I was still out of school and having private tuition paid for by my family until our appeal could be heard. My dad had gone through the evidence and meticulously studied all the documents and witness statements and he thought he had a pretty good case prepared.

At the hearing, the Exclusion Appeal Panel concluded (after a thorough investigation including oral evidence from witnesses) that my appeal should be upheld and that I should be fully reinstated to school. The panel concluded that I was not guilty of kicking the pupil. They also found that in fact there had been a serious case of mistaken identity, or, as they put it, 'unfortunate confusion' with another pupil who was said to be one of the individuals involved. You can imagine that is not how my dad and family saw it, but justice was finally served, or so we thought.

'It was just typical of my dad: when something is wrong he will go to the ends of the earth to find out the truth.'

While the matter should have been resolved at that stage (the beginning of April 2001), the battle was not over as the school refused to reinstate me back to my class as instructed by the Independent Appeals Panel. Instead, I was offered segregated tuition. All this was going on just before I took my GCSEs, so it was really bad timing. My dad arranged for alternative private tuition and exams. In the end I sat the GCSEs in different locations. It was not ideal as I had missed crucial weeks of education but I did my best given the circumstances. Some exams I sat back at the school, but they wouldn't let me go back to my class so I had to sit on my own. The rest I sat at other local schools.

I didn't enjoy school that much anyway before the incident, except for my friends and the sports, of course, but when this happened I thought that everything I had worked for was going down the drain. I was worried, too, that I would lose my racing career and opportunity with McLaren because Ron Dennis, just like my dad, had always told me, 'Lewis, you've got to work hard at school.' Well, I wasn't the perfect student, but I did the best I could and did what I had to in order to get by.

Following this bad experience, and the unnecessary stresses and strains brought upon my whole family, my dad decided it was time that we moved away from Stevenage. We relocated fifteen minutes away to a lovely quiet village where no one knew us at the time. When I look back, I think what a shame my Stevenage school years were spoiled by a 'mistake'. Although the Local Education Authority has admitted it was all a mistake, neither I nor my family have received an apology, private or public. It is much too late for me now but it would be good for me to know that something like this could never happen to another pupil. One thing is for sure: without my dad's attention to detail I would have been lost. It has given me a completely different perspective on school life.

Preparing for my first race in my new kart and helmet.

After such an unbelievably bad experience I was glad to eventually leave John Henry Newman School. I moved to the Cambridge Arts and Sciences College. CATS, as it is known, was a fantastic place. The teachers were professional and the pupils too. I travelled by train to Cambridge most times until I passed my driving test and then I would drive there. It was a really great experience. I had the opportunity to stay at the college, but I did not want to share dorms with people who I did not even know plus I liked living at home with my family. To be honest, looking back now, I should have boarded because it would have been good to live on my own and to spend time with people of my own age who were not from the motor-racing world.

There were people of all backgrounds: wealthy kids and not-so-wealthy ones. It was a real mixed bunch. It was a pleasurable experience for me. The staff were really nice: they spoke to you on the level and not as if they were above you. I also felt more fulfilled and began to value myself differently. I was happier. I liked design, technology and music, but my dad wasn't keen

Happy with another grade and certificate in karate.

on me taking music and recommended that I do business studies. He thought that it would be more useful and relevant in motor racing and that it would give me a better chance at a decent job should I ever need it to fall back on.

I didn't think business studies was right for me – which is probably the reason I didn't do so well in the exam. I was not even slightly interested and if you're forced to do something you don't like, you're not going to do as well in it. I was into music. I played the guitar and I also wanted to learn the drums. I always wanted to be like Phil Collins – he can play everything: guitar, drums, piano, bass guitar . . . Music was something I enjoyed and wanted to do at college, but in the end I listened to my dad. I still didn't like business studies and, for that matter, some other subjects as well.

'Once I went to college, I realized that I could enjoy more things and I bucked up my ideas a lot.'

But I really enjoyed CATS and the city of Cambridge itself. Before I went there, I just thought, 'I'm going to be a bum!' I never said to myself, 'I'm going to be a professional racing driver' or anything like that. It did not cross my mind. Once I went to college, I realized that I could enjoy more things and I bucked up my ideas a lot. I felt like I really wanted to do well. Something clicked for me. It was a much smaller class and I got on well with my teachers. Bar a couple of really smart girls and maybe one smart lad, I was one of the top students in my class. I was even learning and understanding my science studies! But I am the kind of person who wants to be able to do everything. Aside from music, I particularly wanted to do French. It turned out to be my best subject. I almost aced French.

I spent some of my teenage years kart racing in France and Italy and so found it relatively easy to speak French with a French accent and Italian with an Italian accent. I speak more confidently in Italian than in French, I don't know why. But when I go to France it all comes back to me. I want to be able to really speak it fluently, although I can't comprehend it well. I don't know how anyone can! How can they store all that information?

Then again, I don't really speak good enough English, let alone another language . . .

It got tough for me as time went by, though. My college days were Tuesday, Wednesday and Thursday and I had to work hard to catch up on the work I missed, because the Formula Renault single-seater testing always took place on the same days. So I took extra lessons, just as I had done when I was at secondary school when we had a tutor to help me. I had to get there an hour earlier or work later. I worked some really long days to make sure I caught up. It was the first time in my life in my academic work that I actually thought to myself, 'I can do this and I can do well in exams.'

When I went to CATS, they were willing to give me time. They were totally open to my racing. They didn't even ask about it. They were just, 'This is what you have to do, if that's what you want to do then go and do it . . .' They never said, 'Oh, Lewis, you shouldn't be taking this time off.' They never questioned it. Instead it was, 'Well, how can we work around it?' And that's why it was so good. They worked with me.

My brother Nic's third birthday party.

In fairness there were also some good memories from my Stevenage schooldays. I really liked playing football. I started in midfield and I would go into a tackle and go in so hard that I risked breaking my leg. I did not deliberately foul people, or go in with studs showing or anything like that, but I would give it a real sliding tackle and if I got the ball I would go charging off and do the best job I could with it. My problem was that I always kept my head down. I was always looking at the ball instead of where I was going and so would end up being tackled or run into another player. I always thought I did twice the amount of work of any other player on the field but for half the result! But I knew, at least, that I did the best job I could.

In general, I liked competitive sports – I didn't want to read about the rules or go and watch it; I just wanted to do it because it was good fun – but motor racing was different. I read, studied and knew all the rules.

I was relatively good at most sports: I played for the cricket team, the basketball team, the footy team. I was on the athletics team and I did javelin, discus and the 800 metres and won the occasional event on school sports days.

Nic also loves competitive sports but is unable to compete in most. Still, he tries and he tries and he never gets down or depressed about things. If he fell over, he would get straight back up and get on with it even if he was in pain. He made such a big impact on me and on the way I think about things. Nic is blessed in so many ways.

Even now, I am sometimes quite hard on Nic about small things, I just want to help him learn and not to take anything for granted. Most importantly, I want him to do well, even better than me, in his education and exams and so I keep on top of him about this. He always tells me I am the best and he never really talks to me about my driving. He is so sensible.

STARTING OUT

MY DAD HAS ALWAYS BEEN MY MANAGER and my adviser. I remember years ago, when I was about twelve, in Junior Yamaha and at a race track giving an interview. I said, 'My dad gives me advice on what to do on the track, but I don't listen to it because he doesn't know what it's like out there.'

I regret saying that because it's not true. I remember I was angry at the time because things were not going so well. Dad's got a much wiser head on his shoulders than me so he knows a lot of the stuff he says is true. He's always right. It got to the point where I took bits out of what he was saying and then added my own bit – what I thought should be right. I think that's why we work well as a team. We gel together.

At a young age, he was very hard on me and now that I am older and a little bit wiser I fully understand and appreciate why. I can probably guarantee that he was harder on me than any other driver's father was on his son. I don't just mean in life at the track – I mean in life generally. He brought me up to appreciate people and to appreciate general values: you know, be polite and always say thank you, always have a smile on your face, do not be rude – all those things. If I made a mistake in that sort of area, where I wasn't polite, I was made aware of it. I'm easy to get on with. I'm just as normal as any other driver, or any other person. When I started karting, my dad did a kind of deal with me. He said that he would support me going racing, but only if I worked harder at school. I remember my dad had to work three jobs just to make ends meet and to keep his end of the bargain. During the day he worked for British Rail – as it was back then – as a computer manager, having risen through the ranks over 14 years from an admin clerk. When he arrived back home he would go straight out again and erect 'For Sale' sign boards in his suit for a local estate agent. I think he only used to get 50 pence a board but it all helped and every penny counted. In any other spare time, my dad used to knock on doors trying to book double-glazing appointments for his friend Terry Holland's business. It was not a job he enjoyed but he still did it.

The first time I sat in a go-kart was when we all went on holiday to Ibiza. It was in August 1988, and I was three years old. I had not really been anywhere abroad before then for a summer holiday, so I remember it pretty well. Both my dad and Linda were working for British Rail and they were located at King's Cross. I remember they were living in a small one-bedroom flat in Hatfield. We stayed in a mobile home camp in Ibiza and we travelled one way by plane and one way by train as this was all they could afford. The plane journey was something they saved up for, while the train tickets were part of a concession through working for the railway. A big group of us went on that holiday. The real highlight for me in Ibiza was the trip to the kart track.

'The first time I sat in a go-kart was when we all went on holiday to Ibiza.'

They had little electric kiddie karts and the track was very small. It was less than a hundred metres long, probably only about sixty metres, but I loved it. I got in a kart and straightaway I knew I was going to enjoy it. I remember thinking I was Ayrton Senna, it just felt natural.

After that, nobody gave it a second thought. My dad was just a railway worker and I was just a kid. We went home and I thought that was it, but my dad remembered how much we had all enjoyed it, especially me. We thought nothing of it until a couple of years later.

For my fifth birthday I got my first remote control car. I remember them putting the batteries in this little car. I drove it up and down the hallway and tried it outside, too. I really liked it. I suppose that was the beginning, or at least the beginning of the beginning. I was consciously hooked on cars from that point.

A few months later my dad brought me an even bigger and better 1/12th scale electric remote control car and spent days building it up from all the bits in a box when he came home from work. I loved it. I was always pestering him to keep recharging the batteries. Eventually my dad thought enough's enough, if we are going to muck around with this car then let's do it properly and join a club. So we did just that. We went down to our local model shop Models in Motion, in the Old Town in Stevenage, and we joined the racing club and went remote-control-car racing every weekend on Sunday mornings. It was great fun for us both. There were like fifty adults racing and just two kids – and one of them was me. I found I was really competitive. My dad loved it and pretty soon he was helping me with everything. I guess that is when he became my first mechanic.

'At the end of my first season the club gave me a special award for the most impressive driver.'

We used to go to the shop and get all kinds of new parts, and paint, and try to improve the car. We went racing at a village called Bennington with my electric remote-control car packed in the back of Linda's car – a white Mini Metro that cost my dad £100. In my first year I came second in the club championship, having beaten the adult who had been racing for years. They were a great bunch of people from what I remember and the camaraderie was brilliant. They didn't mind me, a little kid, joining in their fun and beating them at it. It was through the hobby shop Models in Motion that I got my chance to go on BBC television's *Blue Peter*. I was just six years old. At the end of my first season the club gave me a special award for the most impressive driver – so with this and ending up on television, what more could a kid ask for!

The next step came when we moved up from electric remote-control cars to a 1/8th scale petrol-engined car called a Turbo Burns. I still have the car to this day. I remember it cost my dad a whopping £250 to buy second hand from someone at the track. I was still living in Peartree Way then, with my mum, but my dad and Linda had by that time moved to Shearwater Close in Stevenage where they bought a small three-bedroomed house with its own garden. It was our house. It was when Linda was expecting Nic, so they needed more space. Dad bought the house in Shearwater Close and let the flat in Hatfield. He couldn't really afford to keep either but somehow he just managed because he had to. It meant we were now living in Stevenage closer to my mum and that was good for me. Nic was born the following year, in March 1992, and that summer, when I was seven, I went to Rye House at Hoddesdon, in Hertfordshire, for my first ride in a real go-kart on a real kart track. My dad took me for a day out following what we thought was a successful year in remote-control-car racing. We knew absolutely nothing about kart racing but we were just having fun. I went out on the little circuit at the back of Rye House – I mean the little one that no one else would dare go on – and I had a really good time. I got the bug for karting from that moment. That was it, that was all I ever wanted to do. It was wicked and my dad was now in trouble!

My first kart, aged eight.

A few weeks later, there were some pretty strange goings-on in the shed at the back of our house. My dad used to sit most nights in the shed preparing my remote-control cars, a job he had done for nearly eighteen months, when suddenly he built this extension to the shed from wood that he bought at the local DIY shop. The shed door used to be located on the side of the shed but now it was transformed into a pair of front double doors. I got my first go-kart that Christmas. I remember I was at my mum's for the morning on that Christmas Day and then I went to my dad's house. My mum was just dropping me off and my dad wasn't in. I looked through the letter box and I could see down the hallway and onto the table. And there, I saw something really big in wrapping paper. I guess I ruined the surprise. I remember I was walking backwards into the house trying to act like I hadn't even noticed this big monster of a present on the table! Eventually, I got to open it after my dad strung it out and pretended it wasn't for me. You know what: they had given me the best gift that I'd ever had in my life up to that point.

'I got the bug for karting from that moment. That was it, that was all I ever wanted to do.'

They had also bought me a pale blue driving suit and matching race gloves, and a red FM helmet. I had the biggest smile ever on my face. We went out and I drove it on the street. We lived in a quiet close so it was okay, plus it was Christmas Day so why not? It turned out that this kart was a tenth-hand, rickety old thing when dad bought it, but he worked night and day to rebuild it in his purpose-built extended shed. He did everything to make it as good as new: completely re-sprayed it and polished everything that could be polished. That way, I would fit in with all the other kids whose parents could afford brand new presents. I was truly thrilled. I was buzzing. Of course, I wanted to try it out properly and, on my birthday two weeks later, we took it down to Rye House in the back of my dad's Vauxhall Cavalier, with boot open, kart hanging out – what a sight we were – but we didn't care; we were going karting. I had my first run on Saturday,

9 January, two days after my birthday. I was eight years old. And the rest is history!

Seriously, it was a real big thing in my life. It was when I started my karting career. I began racing at the then Hoddesdon Kart Racing Club, Rye House, which was run by Alan Kilby and Harry Sowden. I raced in the Cadet Populars class as a novice and was instantly on the pace. If you are a new driver, you have to wear black plates for your first six races so that all the other drivers know you are a novice. Over a number of weekends, I brought home six first-place novice trophies from various circuits.

Dreaming and hoping that one day...

I was now ready and qualified to go on to yellow plates and start racing with the bigger, more experienced, drivers. I took part in my first 'yellow plate' race on 2 May 1993, I think at Clay Pigeon Kart Club down in Dorset, and I won against all the odds.

In my first year of cadet karting I was quite often quicker than some of the older and more experienced kids and occasionally if I overtook them on the circuit they would come up to me off the track and warn me off. It happened to my dad also, their dads would warn my dad off. I was already learning karate and so my dad decided to take it up as well, as we thought maybe this karting stuff is a bit more physical than we first thought. We both joined the local Stevenage Shotokan Karate Club run by Mike Nursey, a 6th Dan. I managed to get up to one grade short of intermediate black belt when I was ten. A lot of people have said I am black belt and I have not really corrected them as it has been easier to just say nothing. Although I was smaller for my age than most of my competitors, I was never scared to stand up for myself. My dad reached the same grade but we were away so much with karting that it was impossible to compete for our black belts.

'In my first year of cadet karting I was quite often quicker than some of the older and more experienced kids.'

We would go testing at Rye House occasionally during the week but mostly every weekend. My dad would always stand on the inside of the circuit at the hairpin. He watched to see where the best drivers were braking and he would go and stand there and say to me, 'You've got to brake here, at least a metre later than the other competitors.' Then, he would move a metre further and say, 'You've got to brake here!' So I had to brake later than the drivers who were braking late and doing well. And that's how, and where, I learned how to brake late. I was pushing and pushing, and lots of the time I went off because it was just impossible to brake that late. And he would say, 'No, you can do it, go on, you can do it.' Eventually, it worked and I could brake later than any of my competitors and still keep the momentum in the kart. This was one of the keys to my success on the karting circuits.

I also had my first crash at Rye House on a practice day. I think it was Saturday, 30 January, the day before my first 'black plate' race day. It was getting close to the circuit closing time and we were just about to finish. We were on our last couple of runs and some dude came up on the inside of me and clipped me into the first corner. I didn't even know he was there and he sent me off flat-out into the tyre wall. I went straight into the tyres – my kart was all bent and damaged and I had a bleeding nose. My dad charged up from the bottom end of the circuit fearing that I had hurt myself, but when he got to me the first thing I said was, 'Can you fix it for tomorrow?' I wasn't bothered at all about me. I was just in a bit of a daze. My dad drove all the way to the other side of London to find the parts for my Allkart. Eventually he got the necessary parts from a nice man called Bruno Ferrari. Bruno used to tune race engines for Dan Wheldon and a few others at the time. Dan was then a huge karting star even though he was only about thirteen. Anyway, my dad got the parts and fixed my kart; we went racing the next day and I brought home my first trophy!

Eventually I competed in events all over the country nearly every two weeks. I remember going up to Larkhall, in Scotland, and staying in this weird hotel where everything was painted black. It was a real scary Addams Family type of place! And there was a place called Rowrah up in the Lake District way up north, where it seemed to rain non-stop. But it was all good experience, travelling out into the middle of nowhere just to race karts. The whole family used to go along in my dad's red Vauxhall Cavalier with a little old box trailer that danced around all over the place behind us. We stuck all the gear in this little box thing, then we put the go-kart on top of it, with all these different straps to stop the thing from flying away. And off we'd go.

When I was nine, I entered my first British Cadet Kart Championship. We had sold our old Allkart and bought a new bright green Zip Kart made by Martin Hines. Martin owned the company and was a very successful figure in the karting business and he ran a team called the Zip Young Guns.

We couldn't afford to be in the Zip Young Guns team and so remained independent but with advice, help and assistance from Martin.

Eventually, we bought a larger second-hand box trailer with a roller door on the back, which was a huge improvement. But then the poor old Cavalier had to drag this heavy trailer around all the time. I remember we would travel up to Larkhall in the wind and the rain, and when we arrived most of the other competitors had camper vans or caravans, while we had a box trailer. Linda would have to bring the microwave and kettle from the kitchen and sit in the back of the box trailer during the cold and windy days with Nic, then aged two, on her lap. That was hard on everyone but they did it for me and we thoroughly enjoyed every minute of it.

By this time, my dad had even got a Calor gas heater and put it at the back of the trailer. So Linda and Nic were in the back, jackets on, freezing cold, and then there was me and my dad, at the front of the trailer trying to prepare the kart. I remember Linda always brought a red flask along, full of chicken noodle soup.

After that weekend, my dad said 'never again' and somehow worked a few more jobs to buy a really old Bedford camper van that Linda named 'Maureen'. Life started to get better. No more cold, damp soggy baps but instead we had toast in the mornings before a race – heaven!

It is hard for any family who have to find the money to race, particularly so in the case of my parents who just had normal day jobs. For those first three or four years, before we had backing from McLaren, it was probably a lot more of a strain for my family than it was for me, and especially for my dad. For me, it was just get in the camper, go to the racetrack, sign on, do my driver's briefing and then go and race – and that felt natural. We didn't always win; it was tough and I'd get grumpy like a spoilt kid. I just did not like to lose – and neither did my dad.

From these early days my dad has been my manager, with Linda in full support. It has really been a family team, Nic included. Occasionally our relationship has been strained by the pressures of motor racing but that is just normal. My dad has been the motivator and the strength that keeps us all going. To be father and manager can be tricky; it is not easy balancing both of those roles. Sometimes, I know I can be very cold and

An early
photoshoot...

just treat him as a manager, but then I love him to bits for what he is and what he's done for me – and he's my dad! It's not straightforward. You wake up and he's the first, or second, person you see and so you've got that natural bond. Then you remember he is your manager too. But it works for us. And my dad, and my family, have made more sacrifices than you would believe.

'From these early days my dad has been my manager, with Linda in full support.'

I have proved him wrong at some points in my life, but, like I said, he is almost always right. Even though he is not the driver experiencing what I am experiencing, he is as involved as me, if not more. He is just trying to do his best. It is a very strange relationship we have because he is so driven. He is so committed but never ever pushy. I said I wanted to race karts and he said, 'Okay, if we are going to do it, then we are going to do it properly or not at all' and that was it. It was either everything or nothing and that is still where I am today.

My step-mum, Linda, is fantastic. I was so young when my dad met Linda that I did not understand what had gone on between my parents. It tells you something about a person when they are prepared to take on the responsibility of looking after someone else's kid: me. Ninety per cent of the people I know that have divorced parents and step-parents have a tough time because one does not like the other. Linda is Nic's mum and what I love about her is the fact that she had Nic, her real son, but never ever treated us differently. My dad could not have picked a better step-mum for me. As I said earlier, Linda is the best step-mum in the world.

I honestly do not think I would be where I am today if my parents and step-parents had not worked hard together. With my brother, as we grow up, the bond is getting stronger and stronger. For me, it's the most valuable thing I have in my life. My dad has been the main driving force for me. The way I am now is down to him. A lot of my friends did not have their fathers around but mine was there for me. So, respect to him for that. He has certain morals and there are a lot of important values that he has taught me. I know some people say he is overprotective, but he has always been committed to making sure that I maximize my opportunities to have a better life than he had. Dad is the one who started it all when I was just a boy. Without him, I do not think any of this would have happened at all.

CLIMBING

I REMEMBER IT SO CLEARLY: me on the passenger seat of this old camper van and my dad driving, the two of us singing together: *'We are the champions, we are the champions'* . . . At the end, the song goes *'of the world'* but we sang *'of England'*, or *'of Britain'*, or something like that. It was a great day. And it was just the start . . .

In the early karting years, when I was between eight and twelve years of age, it was all great fun – the travelling, the competitions, meeting different people in different places and just generally having good family time together – but it started to get pretty serious when I won my first British Cadet Kart Championship in 1995 at the age of ten.

The year before, I'd experienced the real dangers of motor racing for the first time. I remember it was early May and I was at Rye House. I had just finished a race and my dad, quietly, came over to me and said, 'Lewis, Ayrton Senna's just died . . . He's had a terrible crash at Imola . . .' I remember how I did not want to show emotion in front of my dad because I thought he would have a go at me and so I walked round the back, where no one was looking, and I just cried. I really struggled the rest of that day. I could not stop imagining what had gone on. I was only nine years old. The man who inspired me was dead. He was a superhero, you know, and that was him . . . just gone.

In 1996 I won the McLaren Mercedes Cadet Champions of the Future Series and the Sky TV Masters title. After that, we moved up into Junior Yamaha in 1997. There was a lot of talk about which was the best standard and category to be in. We chose Junior Yamaha because we thought it was a better career path than Junior TKM, the rival series. People would say we were avoiding TKM because it had fiercer competition but we knew where we were heaing and what we wanted to learn from our racing and it wasn't to be found in Junior TKM, although it was also a great series.

That year I won both the McLaren Mercedes Junior Yamaha Champion of the Future series and the British Super One Junior Yamaha Kart Championship with a round to spare. That was also the year when I was invited, by Ron Dennis, to go to Belgium, to the Grand Prix at Spa-Francorchamps as part of the prize for winning the championship.

In 1998, I was invited to be a part of the McLaren Mercedes Young Driver Support Programme. This was a golden opportunity to be supported by a major Formula One team and car manufacturer. My dad was delighted.

Team MBM – alongside fellow racer Nico Rosberg in 2001.

As I have said, we were not exactly rolling in cash and, although we were getting by, the McLaren contract certainly provided us with the financial comfort that all young budding racing drivers desired.

I also raced in Europe for the first time, helped by the recommendation of Martin Hines to the Italian Top Kart manufacturer and racing team. I had my first European race in Belgium and it was not a great race, but it was just good showing up. I impressed the people from Top Kart and we got another chance to race for them, in Italy. I did my first race in Parma and in the same race was this kid called Nico Rosberg, now a Formula One driver with Williams. I remember we had this awesome race where I was behind him, both of us miles in front of the other guys. I just sat on his tail the whole race, played it cool, and then on the last lap I overtook him on a straight and won the race. That was the day Nico's father, Keke Rosberg, the 1982 Formula One World Champion, came up to me and said, 'That was an awesome race, well done' and that's when my relationship with Nico started. From then on, we became best friends, hanging around with each other all the time throughout our teenage karting years.

A few months later we went to Hockenheim for the German Grand Prix. Keke, Nico and I sat down with Ron Dennis. He said to us, 'I'm planning to put together a team. Are you two going to be able to stay friends if we have this team and you're competing against each other?' We said 'Yes' without hesitation and Keke created our own kart team called Team MBM. We never really found out what the MBM stood for but I assumed it meant Mercedes-Benz McLaren. We raced together in 2000 and had a fantastic year winning nearly every major race in our class. That was one of the most amazing years of my career: I won the European Championship and the World Cup in Japan. I especially remember one weekend, in the European Championship, at a place called Val d'Argenton in France, for very special reasons.

The week before, I had fallen off my bike and hurt my wrist. I tried to hide the swelling because I was really worried about what my dad would say but the pain was so bad I eventually had to tell him what had happened. My dad called Ron Dennis and asked for his help. Ron called the then Formula One doctor Professor Sid Watkins and a friend who put my wrist in a special cast. So, we travelled over to France and took part in the race weekend. I won my first two heats, then suddenly someone complained to the Clerk of the Course about my plaster cast. The next thing I knew, I was excluded from the event. Naturally, with the European Championship at stake, my dad pleaded with whoever would listen but eventually he contacted Ron to explain what had happened. Ron was actually at the Austrian Grand Prix but he spoke with a Senior Member of the FIA who intervened and I was reinstated. I missed one of my heats and therefore started lower on the grid for the first final but still managed to win both feature races, the second one ahead of Robert Kubica, who is now racing for BMW in Formula One.

I had a bad year in karts in 2001 when Nico and I thought we would move up to the final karting class – Formula Super A as it was then – and try to win the championship. It didn't go well at all. We were developing our own chassis with Dino Cheisa our Team MBM manager and it was tough but it was something we wanted to do for Dino and his team. It was a good learning experience.

Prince Charles came to the McLaren factory at Woking where we swapped a few tips on racing.

At the end of the year we went to single-seaters. McLaren arranged for me to have a test with Manor Motorsport in their Formula Renault car. It was always going to be tricky, never having been in a racing car before, and I crashed after about three laps, taking out the right rear corner of the car. It did not put them off too much though, and after they fixed the car I got straight back in and did okay. I started my first year of the British Formula Renault series in 2001 with Manor Motorsport. Moving on from my fantastic years in karting to single-seater racing was something I had been looking forward to for some time. I had my first race at Donington Park in November. I had qualified fifth. I remember all these cars shooting past me at the start. It was like I had never raced before – well, I hadn't in cars. I couldn't believe just how different it was in cars as opposed to karts. In karting I was a king, but now in single-seaters I was back to basics. It was so aggressive on that first lap it was unreal, and I was like, 'I'm going to have to pull my finger out!' It was not like karting, where you could just roll around the paddock and have some fun, get in the kart and drive. You had to be there paying attention to all the data, working with the engineers and all that stuff.

In 2002 I had quite tough times through the Formula Renault days and there were moments when I would come home and my dad was on at me for one thing or another. I was having problems keeping up at school, I was struggling. Actually, there was a point where I asked myself, 'Am I going to be able to do this?' I remember sitting with my dad in the car, telling him that I wanted to stop. My dad is very emotional about my racing and, being peed off, he just said, 'Yeah, okay, we'll just stop.' He didn't really mean it, but I was doubting myself, not feeling that I was the man at all. But things changed: from that low point in my life I got myself together, won some races and then came third in my first full year of Formula Renault.

The next year, 2003, I had a slow start before something just clicked, and then I just blew everyone away. I won ten races out of fifteen that season. I came second in two of them and third in one and because I had won the championship, I did not have to race the last two races. It was such a great year with Manor Motorsport's Formula Renault team that

I decided I wanted to stay with Manor and move up into the British Formula Three series with them for a couple of end-of-season races. From the first time in the car I was quick and setting the pace but I had much to learn. Although my pace was good the races didn't quite finish as I expected. I had a huge shunt at Brands Hatch where I had the misfortune of being involved in someone else's accident but, that aside, I had a fantastic time.

'The next year, 2003, I had a slow start before something just clicked, and then I just blew everyone away.'

For 2004, the team decided to move from the British Formula Three series to the Formula Three Euroseries with me as their driver. I did okay but it was the absolutely worst year of my racing career both because of the car and my relationship with the team. It was obviously difficult for the team as it was their first year in the championship and neither they nor I had ever raced on most of the European circuits before. It was a huge learning curve for us all, but I did feel that I was the one being blamed for poor results. It did cause quite a lot of tension between the team, me and my dad. In what I felt were very challenging circumstances, I won one race and finished fifth overall. This was a very frustrating period. Towards the end of that year, I had a really, really difficult time when we fell out of contract with McLaren. We were unhappy about the year we had just had and this was part of the reason that we had a disagreement over where I should race in 2005. I wanted to move on but McLaren recommended that I stay another year in Formula Three with Manor. This was not what I wanted. I had given it much thought over the previous few months and had also discussed it with my family and I eventually decided that I was prepared to give up my contract with McLaren rather than stay for another year. McLaren couldn't see it at the time and told me to go away at the end of 2004 and analyse my next move.

I had been at Manor Motorsport for three years and thought it was a good time to move on. I wanted to go somewhere else and learn from other people. I thought I could do that in GP2. McLaren disagreed. So we came out of contract.

My last two races of 2004 were to be in Macau and Bahrain and, as I was now without McLaren, I had to find my own sponsorship money to get there. I was going through a tough time with everything in my life. The team I had always wanted to be a part of had cancelled my contract because of a disagreement about the next step in my career. My dad and I then set about finding sponsorship money. My girlfriend at the time, Jodia, said, 'Hey, my dad owns this company in Hong Kong, and he would love to sponsor you.' I told her there was no way I wanted her to do that, but she went and sorted it out anyway. Basically, Jo's dad paid for my racing in Macau. It was a last attempt for me to make an impression in the world of Formula Three. So I went to Macau and won the first race with Jo's dad's company livery on my car but unfortunately crashed out on the second lap of the main race having started from pole position. It was one of the most disappointing races of my life. I thought the whole world had folded in on me and that was it – the end.

My dad was devastated because here we were with no McLaren Mercedes-Benz contract, no money, and no takers. The following weekend we were in Bahrain for the Formula Three Superprix, which was the last race of the year for Formula Three. The Manor Motorsport team actually funded this race which was much appreciated and pretty incredible considering the tough year we'd had until then and I remain grateful to all the guys at Manor Motorsport. In qualifying, I made a huge mistake. I ended up twenty-second on the grid after damaging my rear floor on the kerb. It was a really low point. My dad was unhappy that I had possibly just blown a great opportunity to shine after the disappointment of Macau. We were both devastated but my dad in particular because as usual he felt responsible for everything, the loss of McLaren, the situation we were in, and he was worried about where he would find the money to keep my career going and to fund the following year's racing. He was so depressed and worried that he booked an early flight home so that he could make better use of his time making calls and focusing on getting help. I know he was really feeling the pressure because I had no sponsor and at that stage not enough good performances to attract new ones. Before he left, he made sure I knew all about it, leaving me to kick myself for the rest of that day and all night.

I woke up in the morning with a fresh head and feeling more determined than ever. For the Sunday race, my dad had the team stick his company name on the side of the car. The company was called Hedge-Connect. Hedge-Connect was a disaster recovery business and it was incredibly appropriate as I eventually found out. I started the first race twenty-second on the grid and finished eleventh. In the second and main race, I started eleventh and finished first. I couldn't believe it – from nothing I had triumphed. It was awesome. Afterwards, I called my dad and he was stunned. No one could believe it – I had come from twenty-second in the first race to win in the main race. The racing magazines called it my 'Bahrain Transplant' and a transplant it certainly was. From a bad weekend in Macau to winning unexpectedly in Bahrain, everything had changed instantly, as it can do in motor racing. In karting, I had won from the back many times, but to do it in a single-seater . . . it just does not happen. I stayed in Bahrain that night with my team and it was great. The next thing

My F3 win in Bahrain, from the back, was an important statement of intent for me.

I knew, Martin Whitmarsh from McLaren got on the phone to congratulate me and said, 'We'll discuss where we can go from here.' That was typical of Martin and Ron, they were always there somewhere in the background keeping an eye on me. They really cared and wanted to help but also wanted us to learn the hard way.

'The win I enjoyed the most was at Monaco, a track where I had always wanted to race.'

Throughout my time supported by McLaren Mercedes, a lot of people, and not only some of my competitors, disliked me for the fact that I had this McLaren contract at such a young age. Some people wanted what I had and thought it was easy for me because my racing was fully funded. But keeping a sponsor like McLaren, the biggest company in Formula One, was not exactly easy. Imagine having Ron Dennis call you, having that pressure . . . I knew if I had any problems at school or if I did not keep performing, I would lose the opportunity. Everyone said I would be nothing without McLaren – but I did not have McLaren for those two weeks in Asia. In fact, I did not have McLaren for the first five years of my racing career but I had still won championships. After a difficult weekend in Macau, I then went out to Bahrain and proved I could win even when times were bad. I had turned things round as I had to and it was a most pleasurable feeling. I do not think for one moment that coming out of contract was just a bluff; at the time I really thought I had lost McLaren.

After Bahrain, McLaren was back on. From there, we analysed all the different options and teams in GP2 and Formula Three. I selected the teams that I was interested in and to help me form my own opinion I went to them all with a notepad and pen, as a nineteen-year-old, and asked them how they could help me win. Once we had decided what was the best option McLaren brokered an agreement with the then current Formula Three Euroseries champions ASM. ASM was and still is run and owned by Frédéric Vasseur. Frédéric is an incredible man and it was an absolutely fantastic team to work for: I learned so much from them. They were the ones who gave me the opportunity to learn how to set the car up and do what I do now in Formula One. It was great, the best year of my life outside of Formula One. I won fifteen races out of twenty. Well, I actually won sixteen, but eight of us got disqualified from the sixteenth race at Spa, something about a worn-down rear diffuser, so that took a win away.

The win I enjoyed the most was at Monaco, a track where I had always wanted to race. I got there and I was so quick. There were two races. I won the first and in the second, leading again, I hit the wall badly with five laps to go and nearly destroyed the car. When I hit the wall, the rear wheels buckled, the right pushrod was bent and the balance was all over the place. The car was really messed up. Adrian Sutil (now in Formula One with Force India) closed the gap and he was all over me. I could not go round left-hand corners very well because my suspension was broken but through the right-handers I was okay. I had to be nervous of the kerbs, but I still won and it just felt so good.

The following year, 2006, we went to GP2, which was a completely different experience. There were quite a lot of people there who saw the McLaren name on my suit and wanted autographs and whatever. I joined the ART Grand Prix team again with Frédéric Vasseur, the owner of ASM. Nico Rosberg had won GP2 with them the year before so they were the team to be with. During the season, I remember speaking to Ron Dennis and Martin Whitmarsh and saying, 'I want to do Formula One next year, I think I'm ready.' They gave no indication this might be possible but said I had to do the job, I had to win, so you can understand the amount of pressure that I was under at the time. There was a spot that I thought had my name on it and I worked as hard as I could to get it. I kept telling Ron and Martin, 'Next year I'm going to be ready for Formula One, I promise.'

I remember that both my dad and I had no idea what was going to happen at McLaren the following year or whether I would reach Formula One or have to go elsewhere. I was performing well at that time and I was leading the GP2 Championship. My dad remained calm about my future prospects and that gave me a huge amount of confidence even though I still wanted that confirmation from McLaren. Then, the end of the season got really tough, as I battled for the title with Nelson Piquet Jr. McLaren said: 'There is a possibility that you could race with us next year.' That was it, I had to have it. The pressure was greater than ever. I eventually won GP2 and thought this is it, it's now time for McLaren to give me the opportunity, I know I can do it.

I eventually got the chance that I had been asking for to test a Formula One car. I remember I wanted to impress in my first attempt but instead I took it steady, trying not to make any mistakes but just applying myself

Becoming 2000 Formula A European Champion.

methodically. The engineers were professionals and experienced, they could tell if I was right or not for the job – and then, after everything, I got the news that the Formula One seat was mine.

DREAMS

FOR ME IT WAS JUST A COOL NIGHT OUT.

A lot of people have talked about it since as if it was the night that changed my life. But when I left home with my dad on that first Sunday evening of December 1995, little did I know what lay ahead. I was ten years old and on my way to my first prestigious motor sport awards event – the annual Autosport Awards dinner. This was a major event that is a kind of celebration of the motor racing year gone by. It was a real big deal.

I was going because I had won the British Formula Cadet Karting Championship, my first national title. I felt proud, of course, but a bit apprehensive, too. The dinner was held at the Grosvenor House Hotel in Park Lane, London. There were about a thousand people in a huge room full of tables and chairs and there were waiters everywhere. It was amazing. I was wearing a green velvet jacket that my dad had borrowed from Mike Spencer, the previous year's winner of the British Formula Cadet Championship. Fortunately for me, he was my size, although Linda had to take up the sleeves. I borrowed his shiny patent leather black shoes off him as well. That night, just ten years old and in that suit, I felt really good, like the whole thing fitted me.

I had started to watch Formula One a few years before that evening, of course, and McLaren were the team I followed. I was just attracted by the colours of the McLaren car around that time. It was my favourite. I was a huge fan of their driver Ayrton Senna. It was a strange feeling. It was that team that made me think, 'I want to drive that car one day.' I wanted to be in that team. 'One day, I want to be in his seat.' I had always followed Senna. When I went to the Autosport Awards it was the year after he had been killed at Imola. To this day I always feel a bit gutted that I missed him by a year. He was 'the man' for me. It was everything about him, but especially the way he drove and him as a person.

Anyway, for that Autosport Awards night, my dad made me a very special autograph booklet, with spaces for people to write their names, addresses and phone numbers. It was all done out really professionally. Dad thought we might never get the chance again and so let's capture as much information and details as we can just in case we ever get the opportunity to do something with it. I still have that book at home. I carried the thing with me all night and, after the dinner, when everyone was walking around, my dad was saying, 'Oh, that's so and so, go and get their autograph.' There were all these different people and I hadn't a clue who they were. I don't think kids at that age remember names and faces particularly,

Meeting Murray
Walker at the
Autosport Awards
1995.

but what they can remember is the number on the car, or the colour of the car, be it a rally car or whatever, and the driver's trademark helmet.

So when my dad said, 'That's Colin McRae who drives a Subaru,' I was like, 'No, really!' Colin McRae was the man at that time and he was also one of the guys I met early on who was genuine, who gave me time. That night, he gave me so much time and he was so pleasant. At the end of the awards presentation Colin, his brother Alistair and a few friends were chanting *'Lewis, Lewis!'* It was incredibly funny to have these big guys shouting out my name. I really appreciated Colin from that day. Sadly, he was killed in a helicopter crash during the weekend of the Belgian Grand Prix in 2007. I had not seen him for a long time, but remember that he was such a great guy.

Eventually that night, my dad said, 'There's Ron Dennis, go and get his autograph.' I walked up to Ron. I remember standing in front of him. I remember being so nervous but confident at the same time; nervous of speaking, but I also had my own self-belief, too. I knew what I wanted but I was not confident that I could speak the words properly. I was un-comfortable to the point that I really did not want to say too much. So I went

Me with
Ron Dennis,
at the Belgian
Grand Prix
in 1996.

You win some, you lose some – it can be a lonely place sometimes.

up to him and I said, 'Hello, I'm Lewis Hamilton. One day I'd like to be a racing driver and I'd like to race for McLaren . . .'

Ron sat down and spoke to me for what seemed like ages, ten minutes or so, although I'm sure it was really just a minute or two. I remember looking in his eyes – and I never lost contact with him. He said, 'You have got to work hard at school. You have got to keep that spirit and keep going.' So I got him to sign my autograph book and I said, 'Can you also put down your number and address please?' and he said 'Okay.' He wrote down his address and said, 'I tell you what – phone me in nine years and I will sort you out a deal.' I said, 'Okay' and he wrote down his phone number. He just wrote, 'Call me in nine years.'

Like I said, I still have the autograph at home and it is odd to recall, like when I looked back recently, that I got Sir John Surtees as my first autograph when my dad told me how much he had won and who he was and about his achievements; then Sir Stirling Moss, Sir Jackie Stewart and all these great people. It was so cool. I guess at ten years old I had no clue what it all really meant. I was in a complete daze.

I won several British Kart Championships in different classes after that, and so I went again to the Autosport Awards the year after and the year after that – three times in a row – and it is really a pleasure when I go now because you sit there amongst all these youngsters and you say, 'That was me many years ago!' It is weird because when you are that age people say, 'I remember when I was your age . . .' and all that. And now I am sitting here, and I am only twenty-three, but I am looking at the kids and I am thinking 'Wow, ten years ago . . .'

A few weeks after my third visit to the Autosport Awards, Ron Dennis's secretary, Justine, called my dad on his mobile phone. 'Hello, Anthony, Ron would like to talk to you.' My dad couldn't believe he had called. He came to me and said, 'Ron Dennis has called – and he's offered to support your career financially, technically and whatever is necessary.' I was like, 'Oh, yeah. Great.' And I just went upstairs to my room and got on with my homework – I think I was in shock! It was so unbelievable. I struggled to take it in – until my dad said he was actually going to meet with Ron later in the week.

Ron used to come to some of the kart races because he was the sponsor of the McLaren Mercedes Champions of the Future Series. I remember him coming to speak to me after I won the Cadet Championship. He smiled at me and he just said, 'It's nice to see you up here.' That was, I think, in 1996.

When I won Junior Yamaha the next year, he was there again and smiled at me on the top step of the podium and joked, 'Oh, no. Not you again!' My dad was happy when he phoned a year after that. He was ecstatic, but, for me, I was just the same. I guess that phone call changed our lives far more than I ever understood at the time, but my dad knew exactly what and how much it meant.

I was very appreciative of the opportunity, but I was not really old enough to understand it. My dad looked after all the stuff outside my racing, just as he does now in Formula One.

Though I was pleased when the McLaren drivers David Coulthard or Mika Hakkinen came to a few of the kart races, and I was obviously really impressed with their talent and achievements, I have never really been into hero worship like some people. There are those who are amazed by every-thing they see around these famous people and then they want to be just like these 'stars' who have become their role models. I have never been like that but maybe I would have been if I had met Ayrton Senna or if I were to meet Michael Jackson, say, but I honestly haven't been star-struck yet. I do not have a role model as such: I prefer to take a little bit from everyone, whether it is fashion, style, music or whatever.

One person who does stand out for me though is Muhammad Ali. I have never met him but would love to. When I see him on TV, I think 'Whoah, this dude . . .' He is my favourite sportsman ever. I go onto the internet and watch clips of him and I have also got the *When We Were Kings* DVD. Seeing him in the 'Rumble in the Jungle' . . . oof . . . that was sick! I love watching those kind of old-school things when you try to understand what was going on back then. How cool was Ali! I would love to be like that. No one had the balls he had. That's inspirational.

The style that Ali had and the way he was such a hero matters to me so much more than money ever could. One of the many people I have met recently, a kid no older than thirteen, asked me about being at McLaren and what it is like. He asked, 'How's the money?' Well, I can tell you I have not spent any money, or hardly any at all, and I have not even seen any money! My dad is taking care of that stuff. I spend money like I have done for

Out in front, I enjoyed leading the field at Donington Park in this Formula Renault UK race in 2003.

the last few years – in limited amounts and for necessities only, although maybe one day I'll splash out on something for my family and myself. Ron Dennis always mentions it to me – he kids me about it. 'Oh, I know you're always pinching pennies' and I'm like, 'Hold on a sec . . . we've not had a lot of money to grow up with and I don't need to go and spend any money.' And that is right. I have a car provided for me, by Mercedes-Benz, which I am very fortunate to have. There isn't anything else that I need at the moment but if there is, it's taken care of by my dad. Honestly, there is nothing else I could possibly want. Dad and I once talked figures of what I could earn in the next few years as a Formula One driver and we could not even imagine a tiny fraction of what people say I could earn. It is just crazy.

'The style that Ali had and the way he was such a hero matters to me so much more than money ever could.'

What difference does it really make? Okay, maybe you can buy more things but what difference does that really make in your life? I don't know. I must admit, I like boats, big ones. My friend has a boat and that is just the most

Playing the guitar, and music in general, is one of my favourite ways of chilling out and relaxing.

unreal thing. It is pretty seriously cool. So, if I were ever to save up for anything, it would be a boat. I was very fortunate to be invited to spend some of my 2007 summer holiday on a boat owned by Mansour Ojjeh and his family – it was so cool. Mansour is a shareholder in the McLaren Group.

You wake up one morning on the boat, and you can just go somewhere else. That's what we did and I loved it. Mansour has such a great family. That's why he is so happy. So, for me, it was a real pleasure to see that.

None of that would have happened, of course, if I had not been driving for McLaren and if I had not been in Formula One. So I do appreciate how lucky I am. In 1998, when I was only thirteen, I met Prince Charles when he came to visit the McLaren headquarters. And since then, I have met lots of people from all walks of life and all parts of the world. It is one of the great thrills of my job and I am truly grateful that I have had this opportunity. I am determined to make the most of it and I believe, just like I did in 1995, that if I aim for my dream then it can happen.

RUNNING

AFTER MY FIRST FEW TESTS in the McLaren Formula One car, I was comfortably putting in respectable lap times during testing. I think it impressed a few people that I was consistently getting on with my job. I knew then that anything is possible. I was saying, 'You know, we can actually win a race if we work hard enough.' And that is when my road to Formula One really began. That is when a real new chapter in my life started.

I had been on that road for some time. I was running. I wanted to go to Formula One. I was pushing as hard as I could. Every opportunity I had, I told them I was ready. Then Martin Whitmarsh hinted, while I was going for the GP2 Championship title in 2006, that there was a possibility I could race in Formula One. 'But,' he said, 'if you don't win, you know, it will make it more difficult to put you in the car.' The pressure was now greater than ever. I'm sure it wasn't intentional to add more pressure but that's the way it was. I wanted it so much.

I had a period during the year when I was a bit negative and I came back positive. I had five wins, six fastest laps and took pole and the race win at Monaco in GP2. I also had a double win at Silverstone.

Eventually, at the end of September, I was called to Ron's home. Martin Whitmarsh was there. I went along with my dad and we were told that I would be racing in 2007 for Vodafone McLaren Mercedes. Well, we were kind of numb with shock. We wanted to burst out laughing, crying or whatever but we just sat there as if this sort of thing happened every day. Even when we had left and got in the car we still couldn't believe it, and it was only when we gradually got closer to home that the reality of it kicked in. The family were ecstatic! We were sworn to secrecy so couldn't share our news with anyone except Linda, Nic, my mum and her husband Ray. It was torture for a few weeks but worth it!

It was a very good year for me and, at last, I had the opportunity to test a Formula One car. It was a great feeling. Having your first test in a Formula One car, you feel that you want to blow the world away and I was really determined. But it didn't happen just like that. It took time. The team understood how tough it would be for me to begin with, so they gave me plenty of time, six or eight test days at Silverstone and then I started to find a real consistency.

My first-ever test took place at Silverstone. It was a cold grey day but the world was alight as far as I was concerned. I took it easy, not wanting to make a mistake on my first day in the job by crashing the car. My dad was petrified that I might push too hard but gradually the more laps I did the more comfortable and confident I became.

'Having your first test in a Formula One car, you feel that you want to blow the world away and I was really determined.'

I remember that when I was first given the job, my race engineer and now good friend Phil Prew was a bit disappointed that he did not get to work on Fernando's car. He was, after all, the double World Champion. I remember he told me and I said, 'I'm sorry that you didn't get Fernando, but I'll do the best job I can.' And all credit to Phil, he was great about it after that and relished the challenge of working with a rookie. He turned out to be so very, very positive and he said, 'Don't worry. We'll work hard and we'll do fine.'

I've heard people say that in the past some drivers used to just walk into the paddock garage and get into the car and race, then afterwards get out and go home without even a word. I wanted to make sure I was not like that. I made it clear I was willing to work twice the hours, never mind the same hours, as anyone who was working in the team. I was asking: are you willing to work the amount of hours I'm willing to work?

I was determined to succeed. I was ready to do anything it took. I knew I was young and I was a rookie. But I am very straightforward and I say what's on my mind. I will not try to be someone I am not. I will just tell it as I see it or understand it. I am easy to talk to and that is important, too. I believe you have to communicate with your own team and the people around you in as normal a manner as possible. The McLaren and Mercedes-Benz engineers and staff are some of the most intelligent, hard working and loyal people I have ever met. We all have different jobs but our goal is the same – we are a team and their support has been incredible.

'For me, working as a part of the team rather than an individual in the team is the way it should be.'

There are guys like my race engineer who want to work that extra bit more in order to win. But they, like any other people, need to be motivated. They need another party to work with them.

I think that you have to be completely dedicated and focused to do this job and that's where Michael Schumacher was different. I had read about Michael and I had seen how dedicated and committed he was. So, for the six months leading up to my first Grand Prix in Australia, I was in the factory every day, from eight in the morning until six or later in the evening. Ron and Martin had basically given a number of people at McLaren the task of transforming me from a GP2 driver into a Formula One driver. The aim was to make sure that I was ready to score a podium in Melbourne, even though that seemed ambitious at the time. I put in maximum effort to achieve the best I could. I worked hard with the team and they paid me back by putting in enormous efforts in return. I did two long stints of physical training and, in between, hours of working with the engineers on the car. When I went home at night, I was finished. I went to bed at eight o'clock. And it was like that for the whole six months. When the team saw that, and how enthusiastic I was, even on bad days, they could see I was totally committed.

Working as a team is critical. Okay, it's not always possible as some-times you have to make your own decisions for the best but generally all decisions are better when they are team driven. If I had a problem with the car, I would always come back and discuss it with my team. I never blame the car or my team and it is the same with the team to me. We are all human, and we all make mistakes. If I make mistakes, I apologize. I am still learning. It is about appreciation. First, I always make sure that I go into the garage, and if it's in the morning then I always say 'good morning' to them all. Secondly, I speak to everyone – not just to my engineers but to my team-mate's engineers and mechanics as well.

I give them time, which is important, and I get on with them well. They do a fantastic job. I feel that for them to put 110 per cent into us as drivers, they all need to feel that we are giving 110 per cent. I know I am because I am committed to the success and achievements of the team. For me, working as a part of the team rather than an individual in the team is the way it should be and everyone benefits from the relationship and shares in the good and the bad times as a team.

I do my best to learn from mine and other people's mistakes, whether I am right or wrong, and I try to take all that in and to mould myself so I am a

Discussing GP2
with McLaren's
Martin Whitmarsh.

better person and a more rounded driver. I feel that we are all in it together, we are a team, and without their commitment at every pit stop, I will not get out that fraction of a second quicker to get in front of someone else. Also, I feel very much involved with them as people. I think, 'Come on guys, let's do this!' Sometimes, it feels a bit awkward because there are so many of them to talk to, but it helps me. It helps me feel real and keeps me in touch so that we can work together.

'I do my best to learn from mine and other people's mistakes, whether I am right or wrong, and I try to take all that in.'

During the 2007 season there was a story going around saying my success was the work of other people who trained my mind, put me on the simulator and taught me how to race. I have got to say that is complete bull! And it was a rubbish story. Sure, I worked on the simulator and used it, but I knew how to race, I'd been doing it successfully for fourteen years previously. I knew how to prepare mentally and physically, and how to race, how to win and just as important how to lose a long time before I went near the simulator. Throughout my career I developed these skills with my dad's help. It is my dad's mental strength and thought process that has helped me develop myself and my application to racing and life.

In the winter after GP2, and before Formula One, I worked like I had never worked before. The team and I did everything possible for me to prepare myself in every way for the season ahead – training hard, physically and mentally. I was really feeling confident about my fitness and working on learning everything I could about the car. So, all that stuff about me being a 'robot' or simulator-trained driver is total and utter fanciful reporting.

Like all Vodafone McLaren Mercedes drivers, I have been helping to develop the simulator at McLaren on and off in recent years. It is an advanced bit of equipment, but they have been developing it since I was fifteen and it is an ongoing thing. Occasionally, I would have the opportunity to get into the simulator and just have fun, and had to take days off college to do it. It was an opportunity for me to learn more about the controls on the car and spend more time at the factory. It was also hopefully a chance to impress the bosses at McLaren and show them I could handle everything they wanted to throw my way. I wanted to be noticed so that I could get the opportunity I so desperately wanted – to drive the Formula One car.

For the past two years, I've had a great team helping me to develop and be prepared for a career in Formula One – my family, Ron Dennis, Martin Whitmarsh (McLaren's Chief Operating Officer), Norbert Haug (Vice-President of Mercedes-Benz), Dr Aki Hinsta (the team's head of Human Performance), my physiotherapist and personal trainer Adam Costanzo, plus all the staff at McLaren and Mercedes-Benz. It was a full team effort.

Preparing my mind – eyes closed as I focus on the job ahead before the 2007 Australian Grand Prix.

During my training and development, I visited all the different departments and engineers both at McLaren in Woking and Mercedes-Benz in Brixworth, England and Stuttgart, Germany so I could learn about the brakes, suspension, rear-suspension geometry, disc-control settings, gear ratios, pit-stop strategies, the controls, the dashboard, the launch procedure, the default procedures when you are out on the track . . . I had to take in all these different things. I had to understand them and the details and exactly how it all works and know them backwards. I took that opportunity with both hands and maximized my potential. I did not just turn up in a daze. I went home and I studied. All the sheets of paper and booklets that they gave me, I read and made sure I understood. I had never done anything like that in my life before, but I did it then. So, it is not about being programmed. I was given an opportunity to learn and I took it. I applied myself better than I have ever applied myself – and that is why when I got to my first Grand Prix I was ready.

Spending time playing pool with Nic.

The only other influence on how I learned to win and learned to drive was through my experiences in karting – and through what I took from my family. I am the way I am because of my family. That is the fire in my heart. We – my family and I – have taken the opportunity presented to us and made it happen.

That fire in me is important because it drives me on. Wherever I am, if I have an idea of something that would help the team, I call them to discuss my thoughts or we talk about how it has been going so far. I might say, 'This has made a big impact here, this has helped there, this is what we need to do, this is where we are going . . .'

There are so many people who work in the factory. I try to get around as many different departments as I can – not all in one day, obviously, because there are too many, but bit by bit I try to get to each shop, like the machine shop, and spend five or ten minutes there. It is good for me. We talk and they come over and ask me a load of questions. They are happy to hear what has been going on. I can speak to them freely because I have known them for years. I think they appreciate it as well.

I knew it was really important to prepare for everything in the winter before the season began. And, for me, that meant listening to advice on food, fitness and rest and learning from it. I worked with Dr Aki and Adam and they were fantastic for me, really committed, so enthusiastic. They helped me a lot and we are like a team together. I could feel that they wanted me to win as much as I did myself. And that kind of support is a really great feeling. It is how I feel about the guys in the factory and the guys in the race team.

Dr Aki and Adam told me about this energy thing – that we all have a certain amount of energy and that some days we feel tired and some days we do not. Well, I do not claim to understand it all, but I know that food makes a big difference to the way you feel. And relaxing properly, not wasting energy when you have some to spare, is important, too.

I took that stuff on board so I was trying not to waste my energy for weeks, or months, in preparation for the new season. I knew it was going to be a really intense year. Everyone has the same schedule, but for me it was important to perform with 100 per cent mental capacity as the physical demands of racing for an hour and a half, seventeen or eighteen times a year, require your undivided attention. It is something very special. I knew that and I wanted to be ready for it.

Most people can just go through their lives and balance everything and it's really good for them and they get time to recuperate at weekends. But I am racing on average every two weeks and have been for the past fourteen years. So, in that time when I was getting ready for the season, I was coming back home and getting to bed early and getting up at a decent time and eating healthily and really taking care of myself. I am not one of those people that says that you have to eat this or that type of food all the time. Obviously, I do watch my diet, but I love the occasional bacon sandwich and a chance to enjoy some food just for the taste when I can.

'I knew it was really important to prepare for everything in the winter before the season began.'

I like to have a healthy balance between work and play. I have to feel free and able to do the things that I want to do. If I want to go to London or see my friends, I know I can. If I want to go to the cinema or go bowling, I can do those sorts of things. But I also know, when I am in a racing car, it is important to be fitter than my competitors. And that comes from the preparations long in advance of the season starting. When you are racing, and you have been driving for, say, forty minutes, you start to fatigue and then your body starts to take energy from your mind. Your concentration drops and you cannot push as much and your performance just gets worse. I always train to make sure I've got enough to go for ninety minutes or more, so when I do a race I never get to the point where I know my body is fatiguing and taking energy from my mind. You cannot brake as late or overtake as much if your brain energy is sapped away.

My life has changed so much in the last two years that it is hard to even imagine now what it used to be like. My dad manages everything and this takes all the worry away from me so that I can focus on what I do best. All my days are planned out in advance. I have a carefully fixed schedule. I have no issues to deal with. I can just have fun which means getting in that McLaren car and racing it. When I have to do appearances, I can tell people my story and enjoy it. I try to feel happy because that is what I can take energy from.

It is a great package right now for my life. Linda looks after all my diary and makes sure everything is booked – and all I have to do is arrive and drive. Of course, it wasn't always like that! But I need to be in the best condition I can for every race. I have to be at my peak and all the stuff I have learned in the past has to come out. I try to avoid making any mistakes and I feel able to do that because everything around me is right. So much of it is in the preparation. That's why I went back to those basic principles when I was working all winter down in Woking, reading, absorbing and learning – and training so hard I was ready for anything that lay ahead when I caught the plane to Melbourne.

2007

I had just finished my rookie year at the age
of 22. I knew I had a future in Formula One and,
with reasonable luck, plenty more opportunities
to win the World Championship. I had no doubt
about that. It had been a fantastic season and
instead of feeling down, or in any kind of pain,
I felt we had a lot to celebrate and enjoy. I felt
proud of the way the team had come through a
sometimes stormy, controversial year and I felt
proud, too, of my family and all my friends and
supporters who had helped me to get where I
was, so close to the title in my first season. It
was a day to be happy. In the end, the year was
not decided by that one race in Brazil, but a
whole championship season.

I don't know how many laps I led for in Australia, but it was a few ... and right there and then, I knew I was just meant to be in Formula One. For years I had played all those Grand Prix games, racing against Nic on the

computer. This time it was for real. Then after Australia we followed up with a McLaren one-two in Malaysia – fantastic!

My third straight podium finish, in Bahrain. People wanted to know how I was coping with the pressure of being in the spotlight. I had worked for thirteen years to get my chance. This all felt so natural to me. Pressure? What pressure?

What a first lap! In Spain I passed both Kimi and Fernando to take second place ... where I finished the race. I was the youngest leader in the history of the Formula One Drivers' Championship. That was so cool.

Ron came to my room after the race in Monaco and tried to cheer me up. 'I really wanted to win this race, and I had the opportunity and the speed,' I said. 'You know, this is one race,' he said. 'There'll be others.'

In those final laps in Montreal I was just trying to control myself. I wanted to stop the car and jump out and do cartwheels or something. It was extremely emotional: to get all the way to Formula One and then to have my first pole and first win in Canada. What a weekend.

Then it was on to Indianapolis, in front of 100,000 people, and my second Grand Prix victory. I dedicated this one to Nic. America was so cool. I went to a Yankees game in New York and met up with one of my heroes, Pharrell Williams, in Washington. It was chill-out time. None of the Americans recognized me!

Silverstone is a breathtaking circuit, and has always been one of my favourites. It has a lot of high-speed corners and is physically very demanding, and the history of the place and the fans make it very special for me. Qualifying on pole was a dream come true. I even got to meet David and Victoria Beckham!

I'll never forget this one – a tyre blowout and crashing in qualifying at the Nürburgring.

When your car is hurtling towards a wall of tyres at 150mph and you are out of control, you have no time to think and everything becomes instinctive. I tried to brace myself, and I was still conscious after the impact. The pain was unbearable and I thought I'd broken a rib and my right leg. I pulled myself out of the car and tried walking away but then fell to the ground. By then the medical team had arrived and when I was put on the stretcher my first thought was, 'I hope I can get back to the garage in time to get out in the spare car.'

After a full check-up at the medical centre, I was flown to the local hospital. The doctors put me through a thorough medical including a body scan and numerous tests. It was a worrying time.

Hungry in Hungary. After an incident-packed qualifying session and an
apology to Ron, I started from pole and grabbed the victory.

I was heading for a comfortable podium in Turkey, until I saw bits of rubber flying off my front-right tyre. Then as I braked for the next corner, it just exploded.

At Monza there was a lot of off-track activity. But we stayed
strong. It was a stressful time for the team and we were all
relieved to be able to get on with the race.

Driving behind a Safety Car in conditions like those in Japan was totally new to me. Like everyone else in the race, I was under a lot of pressure to look after my car and brakes, and deal with the treacherous conditions. My mirrors were completely fogged up and dirty. My visor had water inside it, so I couldn't see a thing. It felt like the longest race of my life.

The way I felt after the Grand Prix in Shanghai was the worst feeling ever. Were my championship hopes over? It was just one race though. And I was still confident.

It had been a long season and everything came down to the last race in Brazil. We had such a phenomenal reliability record all year, but now the mechanical gremlins wanted to come out and play. Even as I fought through the field to eventually finish seventh, it wasn't enough. Kimi won the championship and after the race I made sure I found him to pass on my congratulations. We were disappointed of course. But I went back to the garage and shook the hand of everyone in the team. We'd be back, that's for sure.

Appearing on *Top Gear* in December 2007 was great fun. And so was The Stig!

2008

I remember in 2007 I was going into the final
race and was on the back foot. I really
felt the pressure was on me. I felt the weight
of the whole country, the whole world. And
I went and made several mistakes and we
dropped back. This year, because of that
experience, I was so much better prepared.
I learnt to take my time, not take too many
chances, and just do what is required. You can
always improve as a driver and I am always
trying to do that with my team, my manager,
all the time. There were some fantastically
thrilling races this year, including a final
few hundred metres that I, and I'm sure many
others, will never forget.

After all the winter preparations and the build-up, it was just great to fly down to Australia again for the opening race. It was pretty 'stop-go, stop-go' because of three Safety Car interventions, but I was able to stay out in front reasonably comfortably. I think, at the time, it was probably my best race to date in terms of managing my tyres, controlling the pace and feeling confident. It was a good start, a good win to celebrate.

Melbourne 2008 was in the grip of a real heat-wave, but once I got there it was straight down to business – though I did have some cool moments, like meeting the American rock band Kiss. Good vibes from these guys!

In Malaysia, after a grid penalty in qualifying, I knew I had to have a good start and, luckily, I did. I was soon up to fifth and behind Mark Webber. I pushed him hard for a long time, but it was so difficult to pass him – and then I had more problems when I went in for my first pit stop. My right front wheel just seemed to be stuck! The team did all they could to sort things out. My water bottle was also not working, so in that heat I really felt it, while I sat there for 20 seconds as they worked to get me back in the race.

That left me with a big fight on my hands. I was scrapping with Mark and then with Jarno Trulli and they both drove great races. In the end, I came fifth and stayed in front in the championship – but with Kimi winning, Ferrari were back on form.

I just had one of those weekends in Bahrain when nothing went right. After a big accident when I went off into the barriers on the Friday, I recovered some lost ground on the Saturday and then, after messing up the start,

ran into the back of Fernando Alonso on the second lap of the race and lost my front wing. I finished thirteenth and felt so bad. I felt I had let the team down.

Ferrari were back on it in Spain and, like us, they knew the track inside out because everyone does quite a bit of testing at the Circuit de Catalunya. Heikki had a big accident and had to be air-lifted to hospital. I tried to remain focused on the race, though it's difficult not to have it in your mind when something serious like that happens. As soon as the team knew that he was alright, Ron came on the radio and told me. It was a big relief. I finished behind Kimi and Felipe but it was good to be back on the podium again.

Yes, there are demands on my time – the media, promotional work, the training, testing, travelling and racing – but they are all just part of the best job in the world.

It may have been sunny in qualifying but race day in Monaco was anything but, and I needed to remain focused all the time.

'Just keep it out of those walls ... bring it home, bring it home ... you can do it, you can do it, Lewis!' I punctured my right rear tyre when I slid wide at Tabac on the sixth lap, in increasingly heavy rain. It was like a river on the track and I hit it and just slid into the barrier, touching it only softly, but I knew the damage was done.

That incident forced us to change our strategy and, with the weather on the day, the race played straight into our hands. It was so sweet to win, and regain the championship lead ahead of Kimi. As I crossed the line, my race engineer told me, 'The drinks are on you, Lewis!' and I was just about to reply and say, 'Sure, that's fine' when Ron Dennis came on and said, 'Don't worry – I'll pay for the drinks' which was even better!

Unfortunately, in Montreal I drove into Kimi's Ferrari when he was stationary, waiting at the lights, in the pit lane during a Safety Car period. It was a crazy accident and I could only blame myself for throwing away a likely victory and the championship lead. I was also sorry for Kimi, and could only apologise.

The English summer rain and the support of the British fans helped me at Silverstone. My brother Nic was fantastic for me. Just before the race, I was in my room preparing for the start and he came in. I said, 'I just hope I can keep it on the track' and he told me to stop worrying. He said, 'Remember what happened in the karting days, in the wet – you are the master in the wet' and it was great to hear that.

I had the privilege of attending Nelson Mandela's 90th birthday celebrations in the build-up to Silverstone. To me, and millions of others around the world, Mr Mandela has been a true inspiration; and, not only that, he is a hero. He has fought bravely, suffered patiently and forgiven absolutely. When I met him in London, I was speechless. He is simply an incredible man, and having the opportunity to spend time with him just blew me away.

The race was great for me. I had a good start and I was able to push hard. The rain poured down and the track was really treacherous, but somehow I kept the car on the road even though I could hardly see anything at all through my visor. I had to keep lifting it to clean it on each lap, and when I did I could see the Silverstone fans going crazy. They were there for me in the atrocious weather. I knew I had to finish and win – as much for them, as for myself or the team. I had just come through one of the toughest times in my Formula One career. I felt like the comeback kid and this time I knew I had to keep it going.

Coming to Hockenheim I was in a three-way tie for the championship lead with the Ferrari boys, Felipe and Kimi. I had a good start in the race and I was 11 seconds clear at the front when the Safety Car came out after Timo Glock crashed into the pit wall in his Toyota. This led to a long delay – and while everyone else dived into the pits as soon as the pit-lane reopened, I was asked by the team to stay out. I eventually pitted with 17 laps remaining and came out to find I was in fifth place with a hell of a lot of work to do to rescue the race. I asked them: 'Are you sure we shouldn't be pitting?' It made my job a lot harder, but the car felt fantastic and it gave me the chance to show what we could do, as I said later to Ron Dennis, 'That's what you hire me for ... this is why I'm here.'

A left-front tyre puncture in Hungary meant a salvage job and having to fight my way up from tenth place to finish fifth. It was a great win for my team-mate Heikki, who recorded his maiden Formula One victory. I was so pleased for him – he drove a really strong race. I did feel for Felipe because he was looking good to win until his engine blew with three laps to go. That was tough for him, but it showed that our reliability was a real factor again.

The European Grand Prix at Valencia was a completely new event at a new street circuit, built in and around the port where they held the America's Cup. I was looking forward to it because I love street tracks and felt I could press home my advantage in the championship. I walked the track and it looked really good.

However, on the Friday night before the race, I must have slept in an awkward position or there was something up with the air-conditioning or my pillow, I don't know, but I woke up at around five in the morning feeling awful. I had felt below my best on the Thursday and had some flu symptoms but ignored them. And on the Saturday morning, my neck hurt and I could feel it going into spasms. They were so bad I was struggling to get out of bed.

Luckily, after injections in my neck and some painkillers I was able to move and get through it. The team had put Pedro de la Rosa on standby, just in case, but I was desperate to drive. I did my best, in the circumstances, and I was happy to qualify second and finish the race where I started. It could have been a lot worse.

When the late rain came in Spa, I was behind Kimi's Ferrari with five laps to go. I could see he was starting to struggle for grip. Into the final chicane, with two laps remaining, he braked early on the inside line and I drew up along-side him into the braking zone. At the exit of the first right-hander, he moved over as far as he could. I had nowhere to go, and figured the safest option

was to steer left and miss the apex. I let Kimi back past me, before getting back to full throttle and passing him at La Source. He then passed me again but soon crashed out of the race and I was back in the lead. I thought it was a fantastic victory for me ... until I learnt of the stewards' decision after the podium ceremony.

Monza is usually blessed with late summer sunshine. Not this year, though. Instead of golden rays, we had a downpour of rain that turned the car parks into small lakes and gave us a lot of problems with tyre choice out on the track.

I made one wrong call in qualifying and we ended up fifteenth on the grid while Heikki, who got things right, qualified second. But the surprise, for most people, was the man on pole – Sebastian Vettel, who gave the Toro Rosso team their best ever result and their maiden win.

The first ever Formula One night race in Singapore was a tough one with the heat and humidity and the bright lights. We were all fighting jet lag even though we were still trying to live on European time and going to bed in the small hours of the morning. It meant we were getting up late, too, of course, because the driving all took place in the afternoons and evenings. Actually, it was all a bit surreal.

In the end, the outcome was decided by a few strange things happening – like two Safety Car interventions and a pit-stop incident for Felipe. I was satisfied to finish third, on the podium, with some good points.

Too much too soon. My worst start of the year – and boy did I pay for it! In Japan I thought I'd have a chance to jump Kimi into Turn One but my tyres and brakes were too cold and I locked up and ran wide. I was just being too optimistic. A lap later, I got punted into a spin by Felipe and my race was effectively over. After the race. I just wanted to get as far away from the

circuit as I could. It was my mistake and mine alone and I was furious with myself. But I now think the result in Fuji was a good lesson – more than anything, it taught me the benefit of patience and showed me the bigger picture of the world championship. And I think my strong performance in China a week later came as a direct result of that.

When the pressure of the championship was at its height, I drew real comfort from having my whole family at the track in Shanghai. It was my mum Carmen's first race since the disappointment of Canada back in June. My mum and step-mum Linda have always made sacrifices for me and I am so happy that I'm now able to repay them in whatever way I can. And my brother Nic is always there for me. He's one guy I can totally trust and who always puts a smile on my face. Winning in Shanghai was a near-perfect result for me and the team.

'Do I have it? Do I have it?' It was only when I was past the chequered flag and slowing down that the team told me I was world champion. I just started yelling and screaming in the cockpit. I could hardly breathe. Formula One World Champion 2008 – exactly what dreams are made of!

Felipe was a great rival all season. He had a fantastic year and drove like a true champion in Brazil. I know exactly how he was feeling on that podium as I'd experienced the same thing the year before. My heart, and that of my family, went out to him and his family. But he's a fighter and he'll come back stronger, just as I did. I'm sure we'll have plenty more battles together next season.

ACKNOWLEDGEMENTS

This Special Celebration Edition of *My Story* contains new words and images covering my first two years in Grand Prix racing. I hope my story is inspirational for those who want to know more about me and how I made it to Formula One.

From karting aged 8, through winning in GP2 aged 21, to my incredible jump to a Vodafone McLaren Mercedes Formula One race seat aged 22, and now the youngest-ever Formula One World Champion aged 23 – *My Story* is an account of my racing life to date. I am far too young to have a full autobiography but I hope that this book can inspire others to live their dreams. The journey from dreaming to actual fulfilment has been incredible and I just wanted to share this with you now when it means the most – and not wait until I am older and retired!

If one person young or old can find hope and inspiration from the realisation of my dream, then I will have achieved more than I ever thought possible. 2008 Formula One World Champion, and the youngest ever – how crazy is that?!

I would like to give special thanks to:

The entire Vodafone McLaren Mercedes team. Without their passion, dedication and belief this would not have been possible. From the race team, the test team and to everyone at the McLaren Technology Centre in Woking, Mercedes-Benz High Performance Engines in Brixworth and Mercedes-Benz in Stuttgart.

Ron Dennis, Martin Whitmarsh and Norbert Haug. Their vision and belief to give a young 13-year-old an opportunity in life was very special.

Heikki, a great friend and teammate.

The Sponsors and Partners.

Absolute Taste and all the Brand Centre logistics crew.

My friends.

Tim Collings and his team for assisting me in the writing.

Finally, a very, very special thank you to my family – we did it!

Lewis Hamilton, November 2008

PICTURE CREDITS

From this book's royalty earnings a substantial donation will be paid to
The Lewis Hamilton Foundation, a trust set up to provide charitable
funding for children and young people. For more details on The Lewis
Hamilton Foundation, please go to www.lewishamilton.com/charity.

First published in 2007 by
HarperSport
an imprint of HarperCollins

This Special Celebration Edition 2008

© Lewis Hamilton 2007, 2008

1

A CIP catalogue record for this book is
available from the British Library

ISBN-13 978-0-00-731135-4
ISBN-10 0-00-731135-4

Printed and bound in Great Britain by
Butler, Tanner and Dennis Ltd, Frome

www.harpercollins.co.uk